Patricia F. Lehman

Cairn
Terriers

Everything About Purchase,
Care, Nutrition, Grooming,
Behavior, and Training

BARRON'S

CONTENTS

UNDERSTANDING YOUR CAIRN TERRIER

From the heather-covered hills of the Scottish Highlands to their new home in America, Cairn Terriers have charmed fanciers with their intelligence, courage, and heart of gold.

Scotland's Earth Dogs

Recognized as one of Scotland's earliest working dogs, the Cairn Terrier originated on the heather-covered hills of the northwest Highlands and the rugged and remote Isle of Skye in the Hebrides. Dogs that closely resembled the Cairn have been identified as a distinct group on the misty isle for more than two hundred years. Called Scotch or Highland Terriers, Skye or Skye Otter Terriers, Todhunters (tod is a Scottish word for fox), or even Fox Terriers, these forerunners of the present-day Cairn Terrier quickly gained a reputation for courage and determination.

Bred solely for their ability to do the job required of them rather than physical appearance or type, Scotland's native earth dogs played a key role in the lives of the men who worked

The Cairn's name derives from the Scottish cairns, or rock piles, that marked graves and property boundaries.

them. Along the country's northwestern shores— a desolate region known for its long coastline edged with rocky cliffs—wildlife abounded, and small animals sought refuge within the crevices of enormous boulders. It was also a custom among early inhabitants to assemble piles of stones, or *cairns*, for use as grave markers, property boundaries, and landmarks. These distinctive sentinels, inert to the casual observer, teemed with secret life as a variety of small mammals nestled into their hiding places.

Hunters who lived in isolated areas that bordered the Atlantic Ocean used their small, shaggy-haired terriers to rout otters and badgers—valued for their skins—from their shelter in cliffs and cairns. Landowners who raised sheep for the profitable wool trade, headquartered at Inverness, also utilized the dogs to drive out foxes that often killed their lambs. In addition, many outlying districts employed itinerant todhunters, or *brocaires*, who used packs of terriers to rid the countryside of vermin.

Working closely with their masters, and occasionally a hound or two that tracked by scent, these valiant canines followed their quarry into passages so small and twisting that no man could enter. Neither could the stones be moved; the smallest weighed two or three tons. Alone, but unafraid, the terrier penetrated the dark corridors in search of his prey. The dog's responsibility was not to kill the animal—or even to engage it in battle—but to flush it from its lair so it could be snared or shot by the keeper. Few terriers retreated without their prizes and many a "game little bit of dogflesh" carried the scars of his efforts.

The Great Clan Kennels

Nearly every laird possessed his kennel of terriers in mid-nineteenth-century Scotland. Strains developed by the MacLeod, MacDonald, and MacKinnon families, according to early breeding records, figure prominently in the background of the Cairn Terrier. Captain MacLeod, of Drynoch, and Captain MacDonald, of Waternish, were avid sportsmen on the Isle of Skye. MacDonald, who admitted he would wait at the cairns all night for an otter, bred his Waternish terriers solely for their working ability, and preferred a "smart, plucky" mate regardless of his appearance. MacLeod's

Drynoch terriers, with their distinctive prick ears, stand behind many of the early British champions. Martin MacKinnon's family, of Kilbride and Kyle, also maintained a notable line, descended from the prized strain established by Farquhar Kelly in the seventeenth century. Although a Scotsman would never part with his best dogs, as the untamed north became more accessible to outsiders, puppies eventually made their way into the homes of admirers. In fact, several individuals who later judged the Cairn Terrier in the show ring recognized the breed as the same type of Highland terrier they had owned as pets during childhood.

In the Show Ring

By the 1860s, dog shows had become a popular means of comparing dogs based on their physical characteristics, temperament, and ability to present themselves in the ring. Terriers of Scottish descent initially competed as Scotch Terriers. As shows began to offer more classes, Cairns moved to the Hard-haired Scotch Terrier group, which also included Scottish and West Highland White Terriers. In fact, the three kinds of terrier came from the same ancestral bloodlines and often appeared in the same litters. At this point, no fixed standards had been drafted and type varied widely among the entries. Judges knew little of the breeds' distinctive points, although each owner insisted that his dogs represented the archetype.

Mrs. Alastair Campbell, an early fancier credited with single-handedly gaining breed recognition, devised the name "Short-haired Skye Terrier," because she felt the dogs were the original terriers of the Isle of Skye. Several dogs competed under this title at the Inverness and Crufts shows, in 1909, with blue ribbons going to Fassie and Doran Bhan, respectively. However, the inclusion of the Cairn as a variety of Skye Terrier caused considerable controversy among members of the Skye Terrier Club, who supported the long-haired Skye as the true type. After Mrs. Campbell and another exhibitor entered their Cairns in the class for Skye Terriers, rather than Short-haired Skyes, at the 1910 Crufts show, the matter finally came to a head. The breed club organized a committee to work with the national Kennel Club to resolve the confusion over the dog's name.

The Countess of Aberdeen suggested "Cairn Terrier of Skye," because of the breed's connection to the rocky cairns of northwestern Scotland. Robert Leighton, a prominent dog judge and canine historian, urged the club to accept the shortened form, Cairn Terrier, which was already in use in the Highlands. In 1910, after they gained approval for the new name, enthusiasts organized the Cairn Terrier Club. The following year, members drew up the official standard and scale of points (see pages 10–11). By the time the first champions, Tibbie of Harris and Gesto, were crowned two years later, the breed was well on its way to popularity. As the threat of World War I darkened Great Britain's skies, dogs from many of the top kennels were exported to other countries, including the United States, Canada, and Australia, where they formed the foundation behind today's outstanding Cairn Terriers.

Cairn Terriers in America

Like many of the dogs that traveled across the Atlantic Ocean at the dawn of the twentieth century, some of the earliest Cairn Terriers to arrive in the United States were pets that accompanied owners relocating to America from the British Isles. Although its precise beginning in this country is shrouded in the mists of its ancient homeland, the first identifiable Cairn was a sandy-haired dog with black points, called Sandy Peter out of the West, that entered the AKC's Stud Book in 1913. The breed became the last of Scotland's terriers to gain formal recognition, in 1917, when the Cairn Terrier Club of America (CTCA) was founded. The following year, Greentree Ardsheal Gillie Cam earned the first conformation championship. In 1927, Jinx Ballantrae, owned by well-known actors Kenneth Harlan and Marie Prevost, became the first Cairn to win the coveted Best in Show award. Champion Tidewater Master Gold made history in 1988 as the first—and to date, only—member of the breed to win the Terrier Group and compete for Best in Show

at the prestigious Westminster Kennel Club dog show. Cairn Terriers continue to excel in the show ring, as well as in Obedience and Performance events.

Canine Companion

"Game as a pebble, lively as a cricket, and all in all a most charming little companion," is how one historian described the Cairn Terrier. This is a breed in transition. Although vestiges remain of their instincts as working terriers—independence, courage, and a large-dog attitude—Cairns have become fully integrated as members of their human family. Cairns are not one-person dogs, but flourish with the attention that comes from being part of a larger "pack." Their fun-loving and spirited, yet kindhearted, dispositions also make them wonderful playmates for children. Whether engaging in a rough-and-tumble game or offering a furry shoulder to cry on, Cairns have a remarkable ability to sense a youngster's mood and adjust their behavior accordingly. Of course, close supervision of children and pets is essential to maintain a harmonious relationship. Parents must teach youngsters that dogs are not playthings, but living creatures that require patience, understanding, and kindness in order to thrive.

However, despite their need for companionship, Cairns are not typical lap dogs. Young dogs, in particular, prefer to explore their newly found domains rather than rest quietly for any length of time. This alertness to their surroundings, along with their range of vocalizations, makes them natural watchdogs. Different tones and pitches in barking mean different things, according to one owner, such as the approach of a mail carrier, stray dog, or trespassing squir-

rel. Cairns are not quarrelsome with other animals, but will stand their ground when the situation demands confidence.

Perhaps because of their close association with humans—even when they shared the crofter's hearth and home in earlier times—Cairns are sensitive, eager to please, and highly intelligent. They not only respond to verbal commands and corrections, but also to their owners' body language. Physical discipline is rarely necessary, once you've seen the look of hurt in a Cairn's eyes that a mere reprimand can bring. This uncommon ability to identify nonverbal signals applies to owners, as well. Devotees have discovered that they can interpret their dogs' emotions by watching their actions—especially the carriage of their expressive, upright ears.

Cairns may have difficulty achieving top scores in Obedience trials because of their creative and amusing antics, but the dogs are highly intelligent and capable of learning almost any feat their owners care to teach them. "The more time a person spends with a Cairn Terrier, the more personality and intelligence he will display," claims longtime breeder and canine author Betty E. Marcum. She adds, "I have seen Cairns do uncanny things that definitely bespeak greater intelligence than mankind attributes to 'dumb' animals."

These qualities, and many others, have led owners to unanimously avow: After you've owned a Cairn Terrier with the true temperament of the breed, you'll never choose another dog.

The Breed Standard

To preserve the characteristics of Scotland's original working terriers, the first breed standard adopted by the Cairn Terrier Club of America, in 1917, closely followed the one approved six years earlier by The Kennel Club of Great Britain. The CTCA approved the current standard, listed below, on May 10, 1938.

General Appearance—That of an active, game, hardy, small working terrier of the short-legged class; very free in its movements, strongly but not heavily built, standing well forward on its forelegs, deep in the ribs, well coupled with strong hindquarters and presenting a well-proportioned build with a medium length of back, having a hard, weather-resisting coat; head shorter and wider than any other terrier and well furnished with hair, giving a general foxy expression.

Head—*Skull*—Broad in proportion to length with a decided stop and well furnished with hair on the top of the head, which may be somewhat softer than the body coat. *Muzzle*—Strong but not too long or heavy. *Teeth*—Large, mouth neither overshot nor undershot. *Nose*—Black. *Eyes*—Set wide apart, rather sunken, with shaggy eyebrows, medium in size, hazel or dark hazel in color, depending on body color, with a keen terrier expression. *Ears*—Small, pointed, well carried erectly, set wide apart on the side of the head. Free from long hairs.

Tail—In proportion to head, well furnished with hair but not feathery. Carried gaily but must not curl over back. Set on at back level.

Body—Well-muscled, strong, active body with well-sprung, deep ribs, coupled to strong hindquarters, with a level back of medium length, giving an impression of strength and activity without heaviness.

Shoulders, Legs, and Feet—A sloping shoulder, medium length of leg, good but not too heavy bone; forelegs should not be out at elbows, and be perfectly straight, but forefeet may be slightly turned out. Forefeet larger than hind feet. Legs must be covered with hard hair. Pads should be thick and strong and dog should stand well up on its feet.

Coat—Hard and weather-resistant. Must be double-coated with profuse harsh outer coat and short, soft, close furry undercoat.

Color—May be of any color except white. Dark ears, muzzle, and tail tip are desirable.

Ideal Size—Involves the weight, the height at the withers, and the length of body. Weight for bitches, 13 pounds; for dogs, 14 pounds. Height at the withers—bitches, 9½ inches; dogs, 10 inches. Length of body from 14¼ to 15 inches from the front of the chest to back of hindquarters. The dog must be of balanced proportions and appear neither leggy nor too low to ground; and neither too short nor too long

in body. Weight and measurements are for matured dogs at two years of age. Older dogs may weigh slightly in excess and growing dogs may be under these weights and measurements.

Condition—Dogs should be shown in good hard flesh, well muscled, and neither too fat nor thin. Should be in full good coat with plenty of head furnishings, be clean, combed, brushed and tidied up on ears, tail, feet, and general outline. Should move freely and easily on a loose lead, should not cringe on being handled, should stand up on their toes and show with marked terrier characteristics.

FAULTS

1. *Skull*—Too narrow in skull.

2. *Muzzle*—Too long and heavy a foreface; mouth overshot or undershot.

3. *Eyes*—Too large, prominent, yellow, and ringed are all objectionable.

4. *Ears*—Too large, round at points, set too close together, set too high on the head; heavily covered with hair.

5. *Legs and Feet*—Too light or too heavy bone. Crooked forelegs or out at elbow. Thin, ferrety feet; feet let down on the heel or too open and spread. Too high or too low on the leg.

6. *Body*—Too short back and compact a body, hampering quickness of movement and turning ability. Too long, weedy, and snaky a body, giving an impression of weakness. Tail set on too low. Back not level.

7. *Coat*—Open coats, blousy coats, too short or dead coats, lack of sufficient undercoat, lack of head furnishings, lack of hard hair on the legs. Silkiness or curliness. A slight wave permissible.

8. *Nose*—Flesh or light-colored nose.

9. *Color*—White on chest, feet, or other parts of body.

CONSIDERATIONS BEFORE YOU BUY

The Cairn's compact size, charming but feisty temperament, and alert intelligence make this terrier a popular choice for an ever-growing number of families.

When a scruffy Cairn Terrier joined the Ricardo family after following Little Ricky home one day, viewers of the popular *I Love Lucy* television series reveled as the puppy's mischief rivaled that of his red-haired mistress. Problems with neighbors and frequent disappearances led to obedience school, where reluctant Fred finally earned his diploma. Although Hollywood productions have promoted spur-of-the-moment pet ownership on TV, as well as in the movies, the decision to acquire a Cairn Terrier requires considerable thought, study, and personal reflection.

Dog Ownership

Before you purchase a Cairn, which can live 15 or more years with proper attention, it's important to think not only about the benefits but also the obligations involved in owning a dog. To help you decide whether a Cairn, or any breed, is right for you, ask yourself the following questions:

Why Do I Want a Dog?

People own Cairns for reasons as diverse as the dogs themselves: the challenge of competing in dog shows, the rewards of obedience training, the excitement of participating in Performance events, the satisfaction of breeding champion-caliber animals, and, most of all, the enjoyment that comes from sharing a home with a loving canine companion. Unfortunately, some individuals choose dogs for the wrong reasons. Owners concerned with an image, for instance, often acquire certain breeds as status symbols, without regard to

their suitability as family pets. Others fall victim to unscrupulous sellers who demand large sums for traits that, in reality, are considered faults or disqualifications. People also purchase dogs to teach responsibility to their children. Although the bond between a child and dog is one of the strongest of all youthful relationships, keep in mind that most tasks related to an animal's care eventually fall on the parents. Many Cairn breeders are reluctant to sell to homes with children younger than seven or eight, unless assured that adults will supervise the rearing of the puppy. Owning a dog is not a whim, but a lifelong commitment that should be entered into only if you're willing to give as much to the relationship as does your Cairn Terrier.

Is My Lifestyle Compatible With Dog Ownership?

Another consideration is whether a dog fits into your lifestyle. As one of the smaller terriers, standing about 10 inches (25.4 cm) at the shoulders, Cairns readily adapt to country estates, suburban dwellings, or downtown apartments. In fact, one of the most successful kennels of the 1920s and 1930s began in an apartment on Park Avenue in New York City. However, because Cairns are quite active and need to work off their excess energy, make certain you can take your dog for at least two walks each day. Also, check your lease before you bring home a puppy to ensure that your landlord allows dogs. If you own a home, a fenced-in backyard provides adequate space for exercise. Cairns should not be left alone for long periods, though, because they tend to become destructive diggers. The breed's hunting instincts remain strong, as well. Can you tolerate a dog that goes after small prey—even showing off his "kill" to owners?

Assess your schedule before you adopt a Cairn. Do you work long or irregular hours? Have an active social life or travel frequently? Puppies, in particular, demand a constant routine. You must make a commitment to exercise and interact with the dog, feed at planned intervals, and groom consistently. Your Cairn should not go without dinner just because you have to work late. If you travel, you'll need to make arrangements with a reliable pet sitter or boarding kennel.

Do you have other pets? If you already own one or more dogs, discuss with the breeder whether a puppy is likely to get along with adult dogs. Choose a puppy of the opposite sex to your dog and have both animals neutered. Females tend to bicker among themselves as often as do males. If you have a cat, look for a puppy that has been socialized with cats. Cairns generally are not suitable for homes with exotic pets, such as mice, gerbils, or hamsters, because the terriers might mistake them for prey.

Do I Have Time to Housebreak, Socialize, and Train a Dog?

It's vital to know whether your routine allows sufficient time for all facets of training before you add a dog to your household. Can you take your Cairn for walks at lunchtime? Is someone available during the day to let out a puppy? Although grown dogs may be able to wait several hours to relieve themselves, puppies cannot be confined for more than four hours at a time. Puppies need adequate socialization, as well, so they can learn how to behave around strangers, children, and other animals. This entails exposing your Cairn to a variety of situations (after he's been fully inoculated against infectious diseases), such as riding in the car, walking in public places, visiting friends, and interacting with other pets. Attending puppy kindergarten classes, given by a kennel club or community organization, is an ideal way to help a young dog develop self-confidence as well as self-control. Be sure to allot time to work on the basic commands—come, sit, down, stay, and heel—and, if possible, to participate in formal Obedience classes with your Cairn.

Am I Prepared for the Financial Responsibilities of Owning a Dog?

The price of a Cairn, which ranges from $1,000 to $1,500 for a pet-quality puppy from a reputable breeder, is only the beginning of your expenses. Before you bring your puppy home, you'll need a crate, collar, leash, bedding, bowls, food, toys, and grooming supplies. You'll also want to invest in a training manual and veterinary reference. Your puppy will need a checkup by a veterinarian within 48 to 72 hours, a series of inoculations, and neutering by six months of age. Figure in the cost of annual examinations and vaccinations, dental care, medications, tests, and other procedures. Additional outlays include food, professional grooming, formal Obedience classes, and boarding when you travel.

Do I Understand, and Am I Willing to Obey, My Community's Dog Laws?

A significant aspect of responsible dog ownership is the willingness to comply with local regulations, such as keeping your dog on a leash and under control at all times, cleaning up after your pet in public places, obtaining rabies inoculations according to your state's requirements, and purchasing yearly dog licenses. Most communities also have rules against excessive barking (especially at night), roaming dogs, and neglect or abuse. Some areas have imposed restrictions on the number of dogs permitted in a household, and others regulate, or even prohibit, breeding kennels. Before you purchase a Cairn Terrier, make certain you're familiar with your town's dog-related ordinances.

Puppy or Adult?

With his winsome expression, bright eyes, ragamuffin coat, and wagging tail, a Cairn Terrier's appeal is nearly impossible to resist. If you're thinking of adding a Cairn to your household, one of the first decisions you'll have to make is whether to choose a puppy, an adolescent, or a full-grown dog. Many owners prefer a puppy because they want to participate in all aspects of raising a dog, especially if it's their first experience with a pet. Young animals willingly accept training, and bad habits have not yet become established. Puppies also are eager to bond with their families and readily adjust to new routines. Caring for a puppy is delightful for children as well, because they can take an active part in training and see how the dog grows and develops.

However, puppies are not without potential problems. Like other terriers, Cairns are high-spirited, energetic, and playful. Some take up to two years to settle down, so don't expect a lap dog until well into his adulthood. Cairns that are already housebroken and obedience trained make excellent choices for active households or owners who want immediate

companions. They also are ideal for senior citizens that might lack the stamina for long walks or prefer more sedate pets. Let the breeder know you'd be interested in an older puppy or adult. It's common for breeders to keep an especially promising puppy only to discover that he doesn't enjoy the show ring, or has developed a minor fault that would bar him from competition. These mature puppies, which have been well socialized and trained, may be available to a pet home. A retired champion is an excellent choice, too, as reputable breeders keep only the number of dogs they adequately can care for. Adult Cairns—even senior dogs—adjust remarkably well to their new homes.

Male or Female?

Because males and females are similar in appearance, size, and personality, either would make a fine pet. Males are usually more alert and active than females, and some owners consider them more possessive about their territorial boundaries. With their distinctive barks and yaps that announce the arrival of visitors, strangers, or other animals, Cairns make excellent watchdogs. Although Cairns won't start neighborhood fights, few will back down if challenged. Males also tend to display greater intelligence and affection than females, according to several owners who unanimously used the term *sweet* to describe their Cairns.

Females, on the other hand, are a bit more "catlike" and independent than males. Often, they rule other dogs in the household until one of them establishes the *alpha*, or top-dog, position. However, many people characterize them as loving, affectionate, outgoing, and friendly.

They especially enjoy the company of children, greeting them with wet tongues and wagging tails. Females are generally easier to train than males, and display fewer undesirable behaviors.

Temperament Comes First

When deciding whether to purchase a male or female, keep an open mind and don't rule out a Cairn that fits your requirements in every other way. The most important factor in selecting any pet is temperament. Try to view each dog as an individual, instead of assigning traits based on gender. Most characteristics—good and bad—are found in both sexes. Neutering males before six months of age often counteracts problems such as marking territory and roaming. In females, it eliminates estrous cycles

and unwanted pregnancies. Keep in mind that the environment in which a puppy is raised greatly affects his personality. Likewise, it's vital to continue the breeder's efforts by socializing and training your Cairn Terrier.

Show Quality or Pet Quality?

When breeders interact with their litters, they often notice subtle variations among puppies that are difficult for buyers to distinguish. Characteristics such as head shape, tail set, length of back, and overall balance become apparent within the first few weeks. So, too, do the puppies' personalities—their enthusiasm or indifference, friendliness or shyness. Each breed has an official written standard that

describes the ideal specimen. Although it's impossible to guarantee that a puppy will become a champion before he sets a paw in the ring, breeders can usually predict a dog's potential for success based on how closely he conforms to the standard.

If you're a novice seeking a show-quality Cairn Terrier, expect the breeder to question you about your experience with dogs. What breeds are you familiar with? Have you worked with terriers before? Have you finished a champion? If you think competing might be fun for you and your family, make certain everyone is committed to the training, specialized grooming, extensive travel, and high entry fees associated with gaining a title. Most handlers travel every weekend, regardless of weather, distance, and accommodations, to show sites across the country. You may need to provide a reference from a local kennel club before a breeder will sell you a quality Cairn. Don't expect the breeder's most promising puppy, even if you can pay the $1,500-plus fee, until you have proven you're serious about showing dogs. Novices often acquire Cairns on co-ownership agreements, with stipulations about how and when they will show the animals. Others select older puppies or adults as their first show dogs.

By far, the majority of Cairns go to pet homes where they take blue ribbons as "champions of hearts." If you're looking for a wonderful friend to join your household, play with your children, and sleep at your feet, choose a dog that is healthy and sound, with a good temperament. You'll soon understand why fanciers call Cairns "the best little pals in the world."

Color Choices

Any coat color, except white, is permissible for Cairn Terriers. This includes cream, wheaten, red and red wheaten, silver and silver wheaten, and varying shades of gray. Darker points on the ears, muzzle, and tail tip are highly desirable. A brindle pattern—bands of black pigment on a lighter background—also is found in the breed. In fact, an early fancier identified 24 shades or mixtures in a study conducted during the 1930s. However, the difficulty in selecting a puppy is due to not only the array of possible choices, but also to the tendency of the coat to change color throughout the dog's lifetime. Cream or wheaten puppies may become silver, silver brindle, or dark gray; silvers may become golden; reds may become red brindle or dark gray. Breeders can sometimes predict the adult color by inspecting the hair around the eyes or under the tail, although it's impossible to guarantee a particular shade. Remember, after you've spent time with your Cairn Terrier, his coat color will be the last feature you notice.

Locating Your Cairn Terrier

Your Cairn will be part of your family for many years to come, so it's important to purchase a quality dog from a responsible breeder. Such breeders not only are concerned with producing animals that are physically and mentally sound, but also are committed to improving the breed. Responsible breeders plan each litter to make certain they bring together the best possible mates. They study hereditary diseases that are known to occur and take steps to screen their bloodlines for potential problems. Breeders who truly care about Cairns also make a commitment to stand behind every dog they sell.

They carefully interview buyers to determine whether the breed will meet their expectations, and insist on taking back dogs that owners no longer can keep. By their willingness to answer questions and assist with problems, breeders play a vital part in educating the next generation of fanciers.

The Parent Club

To begin your search for that perfect Cairn, check out the parent club's web site (*cairnterrier.org*) for its list of member breeders. The CTCA also maintains a list of nearly two dozen rescue contacts who—through their dedication to the welfare of all Cairns—strive to place homeless pets in their forever homes. Be sure to download a copy of the brochure "Meet the Cairn Terrier," which offers valuable information for newcomers to the breed. An excellent way to meet conscientious breeders is at a dog show—either an all-breed event or, better yet, a regional specialty show featuring only Cairns. The premier competition for terriers of all kinds is the Montgomery County Kennel Club dog show, held each October in Ambler, Pennsylvania. It's always a good idea to view adult dogs, as well as puppies, before settling on a particular breed. Be sure to purchase the show catalog, which includes the names and addresses of participating exhibitors. You can later follow up with breeders whose Cairns you admire.

Be extremely cautious when searching for a puppy on the Internet. Although many fine breeders showcase their kennels online, it's nearly impossible to determine which ones adhere to ethical breeding practices based on the caliber of their websites alone. If you find a puppy that looks promising, be sure to ask for references from satisfied puppy buyers and, if possible, obtain a reference from a local breeder or the CTCA. Make an appointment to visit the breeder's home and see the puppy in person. This will allow you to better assess the puppy's suitability and the conditions under which he was raised. Other sources for referrals are veterinarians, groomers, training instructors, and boarding kennels.

Visiting the Breeder

After you have narrowed your list of possible kennels, contact the breeders to find out whether they have any Cairns that might meet your requirements for age, sex, temperament, and overall quality. Make an appointment to visit the breeder and see the adult dogs before you view the puppies. Are they in good condition—clean, groomed, and well fed? Friendly, outgoing, and eager to greet visitors? The kind of dogs you hope your puppy will take after when he grows up? Feel free to ask any questions you might have about the dogs and their accomplishments. Responsible breeders enjoy discussing their achievements—in the show ring, or in Obedience or Performance events.

Be sure to find out whether the puppy's parents have been evaluated for genetic diseases that are known to occur in Cairns. Realize that your search for a Cairn Terrier will take time, and don't fall victim to unethical selling practices. With approximately 3,200 Cairns registered annually with the American Kennel Club, buyers can expect a delay of several months for a pet puppy and even longer for a show dog. As soon as you bring your new friend home, though, you'll discover the value of waiting for a well-bred Cairn Terrier.

Selecting the Right Dog

Perhaps the most difficult aspect of acquiring a Cairn is choosing your favorite from a group of robust terriers. If you have decided on a puppy, schedule your visit to the breeder for a time when the puppies are likely to be active and alert. Usually, this is an hour or two before a meal. During the visit—and you may want to see them more than once before you make your decision—watch how they interact with their littermates and mother, as well as with you alone. Cairns should be happy, lively, playful, and interested in their surroundings. Often, a puppy will stand out as the cutest, nicest, or most affectionate. However, the one that immediately runs to greet you also may be the most dominant puppy in the litter. These "live wires" usually do best in homes with experienced terrier fanciers; average owners sometimes have trouble controlling them. Don't overlook the serious youngster, which often blooms when he becomes the chief dog in his new household. Steer clear of overly timid, trembling, hyperactive, or snappy puppies. Be cautious in choosing the runt of the litter as well, because a small puppy may have health problems that are not yet apparent. If you encounter someone trying to sell poorly bred Cairns, leave and look for a breeder who raises his or her dogs with the care they deserve.

After you have found a puppy you like, inspect him carefully from head to tail. Are the eyes clear and bright, with no discharge or cloudiness? The ears clean and odor free? The nose moist and cool? If the puppy teeth are in, do they meet in the correct bite? Be wary of any puppy that wheezes, sneezes, coughs, or vomits. These may be temporary problems, but they could signal a more serious illness. Notice

the condition of the coat. Is it clean, shiny, and thick? Is the skin healthy, with no crusty patches or sores? A dry, dull coat, or one with bald spots, suggests the presence of fleas, mites, ringworm, allergies, or a poor diet. Note the type of coat, as well. The proper texture for a Cairn is straight, hard, and dense. It should closely cover the body with only a hint of waviness. Occasionally, a puppy will have a fluffy coat that is quite appealing to buyers. A soft-coated Cairn is nearly impossible to prepare for the show ring. Because the coat lacks its normal weather-resistant properties, even routine grooming is difficult to manage.

If you're uncertain which youngster to choose, don't hesitate to enlist the breeder's help. After spending at least eight weeks observing and interacting with the litter, most become quite adept at uniting the right puppy with his family. Of course, the best way to find your special companion may be to let the puppy choose you. The one that tags along behind you, snuggles in your lap, and bestows his doggie kisses will be the right Cairn Terrier for you.

Purchasing Your Cairn

After you have selected the Cairn Terrier you want to take home, it's time to discuss the conditions of sale with the breeder. Pet-quality puppies are usually sold on spay/neuter agreements, with limited AKC privileges. Dogs with Limited Registration cannot participate in conformation classes for championships at dog shows. (Their offspring are ineligible for AKC registration.) However, they may compete in all Obedience and Performance activities. Most breeders provide written contracts that outline the terms. Other important documents include the AKC Dog Registration Application and pedigree, health certificate with vaccination and worming schedule, feeding instructions, and a sample of the puppy's current food. Consider joining the Cairn Terrier Club of America or your local kennel club. Finally, remember that the breeder is available to help with problems as they arise. The bond forged between breeder and pet owner—and, of course, the wee terrier—often turns into a lifelong friendship.

CARING FOR YOUR CAIRN TERRIER

Adding a puppy to the household is much like preparing for a baby's arrival. Anticipating potential hazards—and taking steps to avoid them—is the key to keeping your Cairn safe in his new home.

Preparing for Arrival

Your Cairn Terrier's natural curiosity, combined with his keen senses of smell, hearing, and sight, will lead him to investigate every corner of his home and backyard. Because dogs cannot distinguish between acceptable playthings and objects that could harm them, you'll need to begin terrier-proofing your environment long before you bring your new pet home. An important decision is where your Cairn will eat, play, and sleep. Dogs generally prefer to remain near family members—their new pack—so many owners select the kitchen for their pets' quarters. The floor is stain resistant and washable, and doorways can be blocked with doggie gates.

To check the area for hidden dangers, get down to your dog's eye (and nose) level. Any tempting aromas coming from the garbage can? Shoes, socks, or clothing left out? Valuables that could be destroyed? Place as much out of reach as possible, but remember that Cairns are expert climbers and jumpers. Leftovers on the kitchen table, for instance, will quickly disappear in the presence of these clever little terriers. Don't leave chocolate around the house; it can be harmful and possibly deadly to dogs. Also, look for any household products that could hurt your Cairn, such as cleaning agents, insecticides, rodent traps, and electric cords. Several varieties of houseplants, if ingested, cause illness—even death—in pets. Be careful with medicines, matches, cigarettes, candy, and alcoholic beverages, as well. Keep the toilet bowl covered, especially if you use chemicals or disinfectants. Don't allow your Cairn near open stairways, unscreened windows, or balconies.

Supplies for Your Cairn Terrier
- Bowls for food and water
- Food, quality brand
- Brush, comb, toenail clippers
- Dog crate
- Bedding, old blankets or towels
- Toys
- Newspapers, paper towels
- Urine cleaner (odor neutralizer)
- Collar, leash, name tag
- Reference books

also might pose risks. Perhaps the best way to ensure your Cairn's safety when he plays outdoors is to never leave him unattended. Stray animals might come into the yard, possibly to fight. Also, the theft of purebred dogs is a problem in some parts of the country.

Preparing your surroundings for the arrival of a Cairn Terrier is, in many ways, like planning for a new baby. Yet, with dedication and diligence, coupled with a sense of humor, you can protect youngsters from dangers they are unable to sense themselves.

Because Cairns will take off at the first sign of potential prey, deaf to your commands to come back, a secure fence or fully enclosed kennel run is essential. In fact, breeders often insist on fenced-in backyards or regular on-leash walks as a condition of sale. Carefully examine your property for chemicals and poisons that could sicken your Cairn. If you treat your lawn with fertilizers or insecticides, wait the allotted time before you let your dog play outside. Certain plants, including hollies, privet hedges, azaleas, English ivy, wild mushrooms, and flower bulbs, can cause life-threatening reactions if consumed. Depending on where you live, poisonous toads, snakes, hawks, large owls, and coyotes

Your New Cairn Terrier
When your Cairn Terrier is old enough to leave the litter, usually between 8 and 12 weeks of age, the breeder will contact you to make arrangements for you to pick up your puppy. The best time to introduce him to his new home is over a long weekend or vacation period, so you'll have plenty of time to spend with him. Of course, avoid hectic family holidays like Thanksgiving and Christmas. These are the worst times to bring home a pet. If you plan to transport your Cairn by car, take along

an airline-style carrier for the ride home. For safety's sake, secure the crate to your car's back seat with the seat belt. Place an old blanket and newspapers inside. To make the trip as pleasant as possible, speak quietly and reassuringly to your pet. Let him know he's joining a family who will love and adore him. Play soft music on the car radio. Once home, let him relieve himself (in the place to which you want him to return) before you take him inside. Provide free access to drinking water, but let him calm down awhile before you feed him.

Your Cairn probably will want to explore his territory, but don't allow him to become overtired from vigorous playing. Also, wait a few days before you throw a puppy party for friends and neighbors to welcome the newcomer. Puppies, as well as adult dogs, often feel insecure in strange environments and temporarily may prefer the seclusion of their crates. Some even skip a meal or two, but it's no cause for concern. If your Cairn whines at night, move his crate next to your bed. Not only will your presence soothe the youngster, but also you'll be available to let him out when needed. Don't relent and take your Cairn to bed with you unless you want to share the blankets forever. Remain firm in your resolve and you'll find he will settle down by the second or third night. Although adding a new pet to the household is difficult and stressful, at times, for both you and your dog, you'll soon wonder how you ever got along without the friendship of this spunky fellow.

A crate not only aids in house-training, but also protects your Cairn when you're not able to provide supervision.

Crate Training

Resembling the hidden dens of their wild canine ancestors, crates offer a sense of security to dogs. Crates protect puppies when they must be left alone, and provide safe havens where dogs can relax undisturbed. Most Cairn Terriers readily adjust to their crates. In fact, many breeders will have already trained their puppies to stay through the night in their crates before they send them to their new homes. By confining puppies to their instinctive nesting areas, crates aid in the task of housebreaking while they minimize chewing and other destructive behaviors. Crates also afford peace of mind to owners when they cannot supervise their dogs.

To successfully introduce your Cairn to his crate, make the task as pleasant as possible. Never scold him during training or confine him as punishment. Also, teach children not to disturb the dog in his crate. Have the crate set up and in place when you bring your pet home. A wire pen is convenient to fold down for travel, whereas an airline-style carrier is easy to clean and sanitize. Be sure the crate is the correct size. Some owners purchase pens that are too large so their dogs will have plenty of room. However, this defeats their purpose for housebreaking because puppies have enough space to relieve themselves and still keep their beds clean. Look for a crate that is approximately 23 inches (58.4 cm) wide by 30 inches (76.2 cm) long by 24 inches (61 cm) high. (Ask the breeder's advice if you're uncertain what to select.) Place a cushion and soft blanket inside.

To coax your pet to enter, leave the door open and put a favorite toy or treat in the crate. Give a specific command, such as "go to bed," and praise lavishly when he obeys. When your Cairn feels comfortable inside, close the door for a minute or two. Speak softly and reassuringly. If he behaves, open the door and give plenty of praise. If he whines, tell him "No!" and ignore him until he calms down. Gradually lengthen the time your Cairn stays in his crate. You'll soon find he enters without protest whenever he wants quiet time away from the bustle of his active household. Remember, the crate is your Cairn's private sanctuary and all family members should respect it as such.

Safe Toys

Cairn Terriers are playful and happy-go-lucky little dogs, so it's essential to provide an array of safe toys. These include durable rubber balls, rope toys with knots at both ends, and the nearly indestructible Kongs. Cairns are particularly fond of fuzzy balls, fabric throwing discs, and fleece animal-shaped toys. However, be careful of rawhides and bones, as well as soft-rubber squeaky toys. With their large teeth and powerful jaws, Cairns easily can shred, splinter, and swallow pieces of the toys. This can lead to choking and intestinal blockages, which are veterinary emergencies. If you want to give a special treat, try one of the chewies made of compressed ground rawhide or vegetable products. The small, easy-to-digest particles allow pets to consume them safely.

Puppies need a variety of safe, sturdy toys to chew on, especially during the teething period.

Be sure to spend time, one on one, with your Cairn. Toss a ball and train him to bring it back to you. Show your pet how to find a hidden treat by using his nose to discover the hiding place. Teach him the names of his toys. You'll be amazed to watch as your dog searches the entire house for his "ball" or "bone." Doggie play sessions not only entertain and relieve boredom, but also develop self-confidence and stimulate learning. They serve as valuable first steps in preparing for all forms of Obedience competition, as well.

AKC Registration

When you purchase your Cairn from the breeder, make certain you receive an AKC Dog Registration Application. If you plan to enter conformation events, you'll need to obtain full registration from the breeder. This allows your Cairn to compete in dog shows, and enables future litters to be registered with the American Kennel Club. However, most breeders sell their pet puppies with Limited Registration privileges—your dog is officially registered with the AKC and may participate in all Obedience and Performance events. Limited registration, which prevents registration of a pet's offspring,

is one measure breeders take to protect their dogs from falling into the hands of individuals who may not have the welfare of Cairns as a top priority.

When you have decided on a name, complete the application and return it to the AKC with the proper fee. If the breeder wants the kennel name included as part of your Cairn's official name, he or she must sign the form before you may use the name. You'll receive your Cairn's formal registration certificate once the application has been processed. Only AKC-registered dogs are eligible to participate in the organization's activities. However, the club also grants a special Purebred Alternative Listing/Indefinite Listing Privilege (PAL/ILP) to unregistered dogs, such as rescue animals, so they may compete in the same events as those with limited registration.

Identification Methods

Few things strike greater fear in the heart of an owner than discovering an open gate and realizing a pet is missing. Because Cairns are noted escape artists, able to squeeze through tiny crevices, it's important to properly identify your dog as soon as you bring him

15 minutes, usually without anesthesia. They also can insert microchips, which resemble grains of rice, with a syringe between the dog's shoulder blades. Be sure to enroll your Cairn in one of the registry organizations that provides 24/7 phone monitoring. Remember, your Cairn Terrier cannot ask for help or give his address if he gets lost. A collar tag, combined with a tattoo or microchip, is vital in helping your Cairn find his way back home.

Traveling

Your Cairn Terrier's lively and inquisitive nature, coupled with his portable size, makes him a perfect companion on family vacations. Whether your plans include a weekend getaway or the Grand Tour, you'll need to begin preparations early. First, schedule an appointment with the veterinarian to make certain your Cairn is fit to travel. Be sure all vaccinations—especially the rabies shot—are current. Most destinations require a health certificate, signed by a veterinarian within 10 days of the departure date. Even if you travel within the United States, a health certificate will allow you to board your dog for the day at the kennel facilities of major tourist sites.

If you plan to travel abroad, find out the destination country's entry regulations for pets. For example, to visit a European Union member nation without undergoing a lengthy quarantine, dogs must have a Pet Passport that contains specific veterinary records required under the Pet Travel Scheme. Hawaii also requires a 120-day quarantine—enforced to keep the state rabies-free—for pets that fail to meet the strict provisions of the 5-Day-or-Less Program. Be sure to verify the policies of airlines, ships,

home. Currently, three methods are available: ID tags, tattoos, and microchips. All dogs need basic tags, even when they have permanent forms of identification. People who find stray animals usually check first for collar tags. Information on the tag can include your name and address, or the telephone number of a national lost-pet registry service. Using a third-party listing instead of your own protects your privacy and avoids nuisance calls from those who prey on people's misfortunes.

However, because collars can break and ID tags can be lost, many owners prefer to use tattoos or microchips to distinguish their Cairns. In fact, your puppy may already have one of these forms of identification when he comes from the breeder. Both methods are safe, easy to perform, and well tolerated. Veterinarians can tattoo code numbers on a pet's inner thigh or abdomen in less than

trains, or buses well in advance. Websites, including *DogFriendly.com* and *PetTravel.com*, offer a wealth of information for on-the-go owners and their pets.

Although traveling with a pet is more complicated than touring solo, with adequate preparation you'll find it a rewarding experience—with memories that will last a lifetime.

On the Road

Most Cairns love to ride in the car and have learned to pick up their owners' subtle signals of an impending excursion. They greet the jingling of keys, for instance, with wagging tails and excited barks. To condition your pet to car travel, start at an early age. Begin with short rides and try to avoid unpleasant experiences.

Be sure to praise and reward proper behavior. Train your Cairn to ride in a crate, fastened securely with the seat belt. If your car has a passenger-side air bag, have your dog ride in the back seat. The abrupt deployment of an air bag could injure or kill your dog. Never open the car door, especially in unfamiliar places, until your dog is safely leashed. It takes only a moment for a dog to escape! **Never leave your dog in a parked car in warm weather.** Even in the shade, a closed car quickly can reach oven-like temperatures that may lead to heatstroke and death.

Flying High

Although airlines successfully transport nearly a half-million animals each year, including top

show dogs, the potential hazards of shipping by air concern all owners. Fortunately, the Cairn's size enables him to travel in the passenger cabin, as long as he fits into an under-seat crate or other airline-approved carrier. Many travelers have invested in soft-sided carriers. These zippered bags also serve as convenient totes on tours or as pets' private sleeping bags. Because only one animal is permitted in each section of the plane, make your reservations as early as possible. Try to book a direct flight and avoid weekend or holiday travel, if possible.

If you must ship your dog as cargo, contact the airline well in advance of your departure to make your reservations and verify regulations. Use only airline-approved crates that meet the standards of the Animal and Plant Health Inspection Service (APHIS). Choose a crate with enough room for your Cairn to stand, lie down, and turn around, but not so large that he's bumped around within the crate during the flight. All crates need at least a one-inch (2.5 cm) rim around the outside to prevent luggage from blocking the air vents. On the day of the flight, don't feed within six hours or give water within two hours of departure. Arrive early and let your dog relieve himself before he gets into his crate. Make certain airline personnel know that a dog is on board, and find out whether your pet has been safely loaded before you get on the plane. The Animal Welfare Act, which regulates air shipments of animals, may be downloaded from the APHIS section of the United States Department of Agriculture's website (*www.aphis.usda.gov*).

Cruising With Your Cairn

A number of charter boats, ferries, and sight-seeing vessels allow well-behaved dogs to accompany their owners. However, the only major cruise line to permit pets is Cunard Line's *Queen Mary 2*. On transatlantic crossings between New York City and either Southampton, England, or Hamburg, Germany, dogs may stay in one of the ship's 12 kennels, where a trained kennel steward provides meals and exercise. Your Cairn won't be permitted in your stateroom or other public areas, but you may visit him every day and walk him in special indoor or outdoor runs. Remember, if your destination is the United Kingdom, your Cairn will require a Pet Passport, or be subject to lengthy quarantine. Note that no veterinarian is aboard the ship.

Trains and Buses

Whereas a number of metropolitan bus and rail lines—even San Francisco's historic cable cars—permit small dogs to ride in carriers with their owners, interstate companies, such as Greyhound and Amtrak, don't allow pets on board.

Hotel Accommodations

To locate accommodations that welcome pets, consult a knowledgeable travel agent, or obtain a copy of *Traveling With Your Pet— The AAA PetBook*, which describes more than 10,000 AAA-rated lodgings and other pet-friendly sites, such as National Public Lands and dog parks. Don't overlook bed-and-breakfasts, beach houses, or mountain cabins. A number of privately owned lodgings cater to well-behaved canine guests. Some advertise in the classified-ad sections of dog magazines. Always verify the establishment's pet policy in advance, even if you have stayed there before.

Health Certificate

Always travel with an up-to-date copy of your Cairn Terrier's health certificate. Information should include the following:
- Your name and address
- Pet's name, species, and breed
- Date of rabies inoculation, type of vaccine, serial number of rabies tag
- Statement that your dog is free of, and has not been exposed to, contagious diseases, and does not come from a rabies-quarantined area or an area where rabies is known to exist
- Veterinarian's signature

BASIC TRAINING

Reward-based training works best with this happy-go-lucky, yet sensitive, terrier. Keep sessions short and follow with a brief play period. Above all, maintain a sense of humor—your Cairn certainly has one!

Known for their intelligence and eagerness to please, Cairn Terriers readily master not only the basic commands, but also an array of tricks that charm as well as challenge their owners. Yet, the quickness with which they learn soon leads to boredom, so it's important to keep lessons short and interesting. Cairns won't tolerate the endless repetition of exercises like some of the more biddable breeds. Their refusal to perform leads some observers to view them as independent and stubborn. A common complaint among owners is that they obey only when they choose to do so. Unless you establish and enforce the rules of proper behavior from the beginning, you'll likely find your dog is running the household. However, because they thrive on their owner's attention and approval, Cairns often lose heart with harsh rebukes or physical discipline. According to Mrs. Byron Rogers, author of the 1922 handbook *Cairn and Sealyham Terriers*, "There is no dog in the world easier to teach, if rightly handled, for he responds to every tone of the voice and when he recog-

nizes displeasure he never forgets it." If reprimanded, the dog's "whole heart is put into the task of remembering not to bring back the tone that hurt him," she adds. Because of their sensitive nature, Cairns react better to rewards—praise, petting, and occasional treats—when they obey, rather than punishment when they misbehave. Positive reinforcement, combined with consistent training, will allow your Cairn Terrier to develop into a well-mannered member of the household.

House-training

The first task your Cairn must learn is the proper place to relieve himself. Although some owners put down pads indoors, it's easier for puppies to master the idea of house-training when they start from the beginning with outdoor training. As soon as you bring your new puppy home, take him to the spot to which you want him to return. His scent will remain and help to remind him of his "business."

Most Cairns—even youngsters—quickly grasp the concept of house-training. However, to ensure your Cairn's success, it's vital to take an active role in the training process.

Monitor Carefully

Watch your puppy closely and be ready to take him out whenever he indicates by sniffing, whining, or circling that he needs to go. Have his leash handy and carry the puppy to the desired place. Choose a special command—one that you're not embarrassed to say in public—and give it each time you want your puppy to eliminate. Praise lavishly when he obeys. It's important to respond to your puppy's signals, even if you think he doesn't need to go. This helps to reinforce your puppy's wish to alert you.

Be Consistent

Always feed and water at the same times each day, and follow a regular schedule of walks. Also, take your puppy outside as soon as he awakens in the morning, after naps and play sessions, and right before bedtime. You might have to take him out during the night as well, until he develops greater control of his bladder. Puppies often need to go out every hour or two, so don't disregard their warnings.

Crate Your Pup

Because dogs instinctively prefer to keep their sleeping quarters clean, crating allows owners to determine when, as well as where, their puppies will eliminate. Set up the crate in the kitchen or family room, so you can watch for signs that he needs to go out. Take your puppy to the same spot each time, and give plenty of praise when he performs. If he doesn't go, take him back to his crate. This helps to prevent the problem of the puppy coming inside and then urinating on the floor.

Accidents

Of course, all puppies have occasional accidents, so don't scold your Cairn unless you catch him in the act. Because he has a short memory, he won't be able to associate your displeasure with his mistake. Never follow the suggestion of rubbing the puppy's nose in his mess. Such cruelty won't achieve any meaningful results. To prevent future accidents, use a commercial enzyme-neutralizing odor and stain remover to clean the spot and remove all traces of odor. Some adult dogs have difficulty

A wire exercise pen keeps this energetic young Cairn safely confined outdoors.

This Cairn is answering his owner's "Come!"—the most important command your dog will learn.

with housebreaking, possibly due to physical problems, and may continue to have accidents indoors. However, don't lose hope. Most Cairns are fully housebroken by the time they are two years old.

Basic Commands

You can begin to teach the basic commands—come, sit, down, stay, and heel—when your puppy is about four months old. However, don't expect perfect performance at this point. Most Cairn Terriers don't succeed at competitive Obedience until a year or two, when they start to develop greater concentration. To avoid confusing your puppy with multiple demands, practice one exercise at a time. Also, involve only one family member in training. Because

terriers are easily distracted, work indoors or in a confined area until your puppy has mastered the command. Keep sessions short—10 to 15 minutes, at most. Ideally, you should end while your puppy is still eager to learn.

When you give a command, speak in a normal tone of voice and don't whisper or shout. Give the direction once, and then wait a few seconds for your puppy to obey. Always use the same word each time you train. It's impossible for puppies to grasp complicated phrases. When your Cairn performs correctly, praise with a heartfelt, "Good girl!" or "Good boy!" Whether or not you reward with food is a personal decision. However, the breed is highly motivated to learn nearly any feat for a doggie treat. If you do use treats, give them only during the learning phase of the exercise. Later, use praise and petting as rewards. End each lesson on a positive note with a task that your puppy can do well. Follow with a brief play period or walk around the block. Always keep training sessions fun for your dog. Never lose your temper or resort to physical discipline. When you train a puppy—especially a terrier—maintain a sense of humor. It won't take long to discover that your little Cairn has one!

Training Equipment

Before you start, you'll need two pieces of equipment: a well-fitting collar and a 6-foot (1.8 m) leash. Some instructors suggest using a choke collar that tightens briefly during corrections. However, a puppy should always start with a buckle-style collar, which is more comfortable and less restrictive. Choose one made of nylon, rather than leather, so it won't feel stiff or bulky. Avoid fancy rhinestone-studded neckwear during training sessions. If you decide to try a choke collar, look for nylon fabric or a fine link chain. To determine the correct size, measure around your Cairn's neck and add two or three inches. For example, if the total is 12 inches (30 cm), you'll need

to purchase a size 12 collar. Order an ID tag as soon as you obtain a collar. Also, look for a leash made of cotton or nylon fabric. Leather and chain leashes are not suitable for training. Retractable leashes work well for casual strolls—and for teaching your puppy to come when called—but you'll need a basic leash for the heel exercise and formal walks. Be sure to allow time for your puppy to adjust to his collar and leash before you begin training. Fasten the collar loosely for a day or two. Then, attach a lightweight leash and let it drag on the ground while your Cairn plays. Keep an eye on your puppy, though, so the leash doesn't become tangled.

Come: All dogs must learn to come when called. No other lesson is more vital to your Cairn's safety. To start this exercise, have your dog sit or stand next to you. Back up a couple of feet and give the command, "Come!" Use your Cairn's name as part of the command. For example, "Sparky, Come!" This attracts his attention, so he will be ready for the signal that follows. Open your arms or gently clap your hands to encourage him to come. You also can teach this exercise by using a retractable leash to carefully reel in your dog. Praise enthusiastically when your Cairn comes to you. However, *never* call him to you for punishment. Make a game of the *come* command by having family members sit on the floor and take turns calling and petting your dog. Cairns love to be the center of attention! Always start training indoors or in a confined area. When he performs reliably, move outdoors

Come. Show your puppy his favorite toy to coax him to come to you.

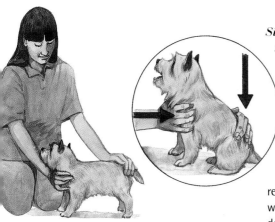

Sit. Carefully push down on the hindquarters while pressing back on the chest.

where he will face greater distractions. Because Cairns have a tendency to come only when they want to, you must insist that your puppy obey right from the start. Mischievous antics might be cute, but if you accept them you'll only reinforce negative behavior.

Sit: Most Cairns learn the *sit* command with little difficulty. To begin, kneel beside or in front of your dog. Give the command, "Sit!" Then, gently push down on his hindquarters with one hand as you press back on his chest with the other. You can also push inward on the backs of his knees to have him sit. Praise him when he obeys, even if he holds the position only for a moment. Train your Cairn to sit straight, rather than lean on one hip with a leg out to the side, if you plan to compete in Obedience. (The judge will deduct points for a crooked sit.)

Down: Start with your Cairn in the sit position, described above. Give the com-

mand, "Down!" Then, carefully push down on his upper back with one hand as you extend his front legs with the other. You also can pat the floor or place a treat on the floor to encourage him to lie down.

Praise enthusiastically when he performs correctly. Some Cairns don't like this exercise, so work on the command whenever you want your dog to lie quietly by your side.

Stay: With your Cairn in the sit or down position, give the command, "Stay!" Then, take a step or two forward and turn to face your dog. Don't stare into his eyes, though, because animals often take this as a threat. Instead of helping him to remain still, it may cause him to move due to anxiety. Hold the position for only a few seconds. Give a release word such as "Okay!" or "Done!" to finish the exercise. Gradually increase the length of time your Cairn remains in position, as well as the distance you move away. To reinforce the *stay* command,

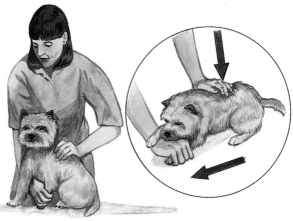

Down. Starting from the sit position, gently extend the front legs while pushing down on the back.

make a game of it. Place your Cairn in a *sit-stay*, for instance, while you hide a treat in another room. Call your dog to you (now he knows how to come) and show him how to find the treat.

Heel: Cairns attract a lot of attention when they go out in public, so it's important to teach your dog to walk properly on a leash without pulling or lagging. To start, have your Cairn sit or stand next to your left hip. This is correct heel position. Give the command, "Heel!" Then, step out on your left foot. Keep the leash tight during the initial phase of training, so your dog maintains the correct position. If he forges ahead, tell him "Heel!" and gently snap the leash. If he lags behind, encourage him by calling his name or patting your left leg. Praise

generously when your Cairn walks nicely by your side. To improve his skills and keep his attention, alternate your pace between fast and slow speeds. Add some right, left, and about turns, as well. If you plan to compete in formal Obedience, you'll also need to work on off-lead heeling. Always practice in a confined area. Start with the leash dragging on the ground, so you'll have some control. Later, when he obeys reliably, remove the leash. If your Cairn has difficulty with off-lead heeling, go back to an earlier stage of training and proceed at whatever pace it takes to successfully master the exercise. Be patient with your Cairn Terrier, and give plenty of praise when he performs correctly.

Correcting Problem Behavior

A Vocal Breed

An important part of working ability was the breed's use of vocalizations to alert their masters to the position of quarry deep within the rocky crevices of Scotland's cliffs and cairns. The earliest known reference to "voice" was found in Oliver Goldsmith's treatise, published in 1774, which recognized that terriers not only pursued their prey by sight and scent, but also "[gave] notice by their barking in what part of the [burrow] the fox or badger [resided]." Today, though they no longer aid sportsmen in their quest for prey, Cairns remain attentive watchdogs with an array of vocal tones at their disposal. However, most are not problem barkers, but warn only of unusual sights and sounds. Some even distinguish between regular visitors and strangers, and remain silent at the approach of familiar guests. To develop your

Stay. After your Cairn understands this command, gradually lengthen the time before you give the release word.

Cairn's innate talent as a watchdog, allow him to bark several times to alert you. Then, tell him "Quiet!" or "Enough!" Praise him when he stops barking, even for a moment. Have your dog sit by your side when you answer the doorbell. This often helps dogs to better control their barking. You may need to set up practice "visitor" sessions with a cooperative neighbor to reinforce your Cairn's training.

Destructive Chewing

Cairns may begin the destructive habit of chewing between four and seven months of age, when their gums ache from the teething process. Furniture, carpets, shoes, and socks become favorite targets when puppies are left to their own devices. To relieve the discomfort that accompanies the emergence of adult teeth, be sure to offer stiff rubber-like chew toys, hard biscuits, or other sturdy playthings. One owner suggested giving a chilled Kong toy filled with a dab of peanut butter. Chewing on a frozen wet washcloth also helps to ease a puppy's sore mouth. Perhaps the best way to prevent problem chewing is to keep valuables off the floor and crate your puppy when you're unable to supervise him. If you catch him with an unacceptable object, give a firm "Leave It!"

factor in destructive digging, so make certain your Cairn receives adequate daily exercise. Some owners fill the "craters" their pets leave behind with water or small stones. Because digging is an instinctive trait, though, you might consider setting aside a separate area of your yard where your dog safely can dig to his heart's content. For a special treat, plant a little surprise for your dog to find!

Nipping

Puppies use their mouths, as well as their noses, to explore and interpret their surroundings. When they nip at their owners' hands and feet, or grasp at their clothing, they are usually trying to signal that they want to play. (Watch how young littermates interact with one another.) Of course, puppy teeth are sharp and dog bites painful, so this form of communication must be redirected as soon as possible toward more acceptable behaviors. Whenever your puppy nips at you, give a sharp "No!" and present him with one of his toys. Praise generously if he takes the toy. Be patient during this stage of learning. Always have a toy on hand to distract your puppy's attention, but avoid games like tug-of-war that may encourage nipping and biting.

AKC Canine Good Citizen Program

When your Cairn Terrier has mastered the basic commands, he may participate in the Canine Good Citizen Program, developed in 1989 by the American Kennel Club to encourage responsible pet ownership. To qualify for the CGC Certificate, you and your dog must pass a two-part test. First, you must sign the Responsible Dog Owners Pledge. The AKC believes that responsible ownership is a key part of the CGC

and show him his own toy. Repeat this process until your puppy understands the difference between his possessions and yours. Always reward good behavior with praise and petting. Never punish long after the fact. You may need to use an unpleasant-tasting repellent, such as Bitter Apple, on items that your puppy persistently chews. Most Cairns outgrow this phase, but some go through a second stage of chewing between seven and twelve months.

Born to Dig

Bred for centuries to go to ground in search of prey, Cairns are natural diggers. With their strong legs, large feet, and sturdy toenails, they miss no opportunity to rid their backyards of pesky mice, squirrels, and other small animals. Not to be deterred by treasured plantings or verdant lawns, these little earth dogs pursue their quarry with admirable persistence. They also delight in using potted houseplants as choice spots in which to bury favorite toys. To combat the problem, watch your dog closely when he plays outdoors. Boredom is usually a

The Canine Good Citizen Test

1. **Accepting a Friendly Stranger:** Demonstrates that your dog will allow a friendly stranger to approach him and speak to you in a natural, everyday situation.
2. **Sitting Politely for Petting:** Demonstrates that your dog will allow a friendly stranger to touch him when the two of you are out together.
3. **Appearance and Grooming:** Demonstrates that your dog will welcome being groomed and examined, and will permit a stranger, such as a veterinarian, groomer, or friend of yours, to do so.
4. **Out for a Walk:** Demonstrates that you have physical control of your dog.
5. **Walking Through a Crowd:** Demonstrates that your dog can move about politely in pedestrian traffic and is under control in public places.
6. **Sit and Down on Command/Staying in Place:** Demonstrates that your dog has training, will respond to your command to sit and down, and will remain in the place you command him.
7. **Coming When Called:** Demonstrates that your dog will come when called.
8. **Reaction to Another Dog:** Demonstrates that your dog can behave politely around other dogs.
9. **Reactions to Distractions:** Demonstrates that your dog is confident at all times when faced with common distracting situations, such as the dropping of an object or a jogger running in front of him.
10. **Supervised Separation:** Demonstrates that your dog can be left alone, if necessary, and will maintain training and good manners.

concept, and by signing the pledge, owners agree to take care of their dog's health needs, safety, exercise, training, and quality of life. You also must agree to show responsibility by doing things such as cleaning up after your Cairn in public places and never letting your dog infringe on the rights of others. After signing the pledge, you and your dog are ready to take the CGC test. Points the evaluator considers include the following: Would the dog be a reliable family member? Does he exhibit good manners in public? Has he been conditioned to the presence of other dogs? Your Cairn Terrier must pass each of the ten parts of the test, which the judge scores on a pass-or-fail basis. The test is not a competition, and doesn't require the precise execution found in formal Obedience.

GROOMING AND COAT CARE

The Cairn's casual appearance is achieved with regular brushing and periodic stripping of the coat. Neither excessive trimming nor frequent bathing is required for the natural shaggy style that is an integral aspect of breed type.

The Layered Look

Working on the misty banks and braes of Scotland more than two hundred years ago, Cairn Terriers were known for their close-fitting, weather-resistant coat. "Many a weary long walk they had in snow and sleet," wrote canine historian Walter Hutchinson, "so that a warm jacket and stout hide were necessary." The profuse, harsh outer layer protected the dog from the drenching rains that swept in from the Atlantic Ocean, while the short, soft, close, furry undercoat offered insulation against the region's frigid temperatures. The coat shielded dogs from thorns, sharp rocks, and the nips of their quarry, as well.

This bright-eyed fellow exemplifies one canine historian's description of the breed: "The Cairn Terrier expression is a mixture of jolliness and wickedness, with that 'varminty' note so much desired."

Today, though Cairns no longer trudge through peat bogs or into sea-swept crevices in pursuit of otters, badgers, and foxes, they continue to maintain their distinctive, double-coated mantle. To keep the coat in peak condition, begin routine grooming as soon as your puppy joins the household. This should include regular brushing, toenail clipping, teeth cleaning, skin and ear care when required, and occasional baths. Hand stripping, or plucking, also must be done periodically to remove dead hair and permit the emergence of a healthy new coat.

Grooming Basics

The earlier you begin simple grooming tasks, the easier it will be to train your pet to accept all forms of handling. In fact, most members of the canine family consider grooming a natural, instinctive behavior. If you have more than one dog, for instance, you'll often see them licking and cleaning each other. Although grooming may seem time consuming and complicated, it not only improves the dog's appearance, but also plays a major role in good health. The attention you give your Cairn will allow you to notice changes quickly and obtain prompt veterinary care when needed.

Brushing

The most vital aspect of grooming is consistent brushing. Cairns require fewer baths when their hair is brushed at least several times a week. Regular brushing distributes the natural oils throughout the coat that give them the ability to shake off water. It keeps the skin healthy by stimulating blood circulation and encourages new hair growth. Brushing also

Grooming Equipment
- Pin brush or bristle brush
- Fine-toothed metal comb
- Shampoo formulated for harsh coats
- Waterless shampoo
- Nail clipper or electric nail groomer
- Metal nail file
- Toothbrush and toothpaste
- Ear cleaning solution
- Cotton balls
- Stripping knife
- Thinning shears
- Blunt-tipped scissors

minimizes the problems associated with seasonal shedding of the undercoat.

To properly care for the coat, you'll need pin and slicker brushes, and coarse and fine-tooth combs. Stand your dog on a nonslip surface for grooming. First, take a small section of hair, parting it if necessary, and brush all the way to the skin. Go with the hair growth to remove tangles, then brush against the growth. The pin brush will help to loosen dead hair and dandruff. Finish by brushing once again with the growth pattern. Next, comb through it carefully to check for any remaining mats—especially under the armpits or around the genitals. Use the slicker brush, if needed, to remove the dead undercoat that is shed in the spring and fall.

Develop a routine that you use each time you brush your Cairn. For example, start with the back and rear legs and finish with the head and chest. Inspect the skin for signs of allergies or parasites, and examine the eyes and ears for

A slicker brush helps to remove the dead undercoat that is shed in the spring and fall.

discharge or odor. Always keep grooming sessions short and pleasant, for your dog as well as yourself. Finish with praise and a treat. Remember, your little Cairn wants to please you. With gentleness, patience, and persistence, you'll have a pet that not only tolerates but also enjoys being groomed.

Bath Time

Think of your Cairn's coat as a specially designed storm jacket and you'll understand why excessive bathing is harmful. The detergents in shampoos cause the outer coat to lose its natural oils, along with its ability to protect against rain, sleet, and snow. Frequent bathing dries out the hair and skin, which encourages doggie odor, allergies, and skin problems.

Of course, because Cairns love to romp outdoors, there are times when washing is a necessity. Be sure to assemble your supplies—shampoo, washcloth, towels, faucet attachment, bath mat, and hair dryer—so you won't have to look for them with a wet dog in tow. Use a shampoo formulated for harsh-coated dogs—and avoid conditioners—to maintain the proper coarse texture of the coat.

To begin the bath, stand your dog on a rubber mat in the sink or tub. Thoroughly wet the coat with tepid, never hot, water. Apply a dab of shampoo to the dog's back and develop a good lather. Make certain to soap right down to the skin. Working from back to front, wash the rear legs, feet, and tail. Then, move to the chest, belly, and front legs. After you complete the body, carefully wet the head. Don't let water get in the eyes, ears, or nostrils. Some owners place cotton balls in their dogs' ears to protect the canals from soapy water. Clean the face with a wet washcloth. The most important stage of the bath is the rinse. Allow the water

to run clear, washing away all soapy residue. Finally, wrap a large towel around your dog and pat him dry. To guard against chilling, you'll need to use a hair dryer set on low. Hold the dryer with one hand as you brush with the other. Move the dryer over the coat until your dog is completely dry. Dry with the direction of hair growth, so your Cairn won't look too fluffy.

Between full baths, which should be given only a few times a year, you can tidy your pet by using unscented baby wipes. The booklet *Cairn Terrier Grooming Start to Finish*, published by the Cairn Terrier Club of America, suggests cleaning the outer coat by lightly spraying it with a mixture of rubbing alcohol and water, or vinegar and water, and brushing with the hair growth. This is an excellent way to prepare dogs for the show ring because it doesn't soften the coat or increase shedding. It can dry the coat, though, so it shouldn't be used for routine grooming. Commercial waterless shampoos and grooming powders also are available in pet supply stores.

Toenail Clipping

Although most Cairns vigorously protest having their toenails clipped, this is an important part of proper maintenance. Long nails interfere with a Cairn's ability to stand properly on his toes, which may lead to a distorted gait, and they are also more likely to snag or break during play. Ideally, the nail tip should not touch the floor when a dog is standing in a natural pose. Cut the nails every week or two with a nail clipper designed for small dogs, or grind the tip of the nail with a Dremel device.

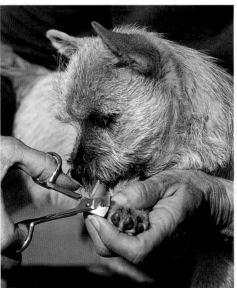

Carefully trim the hair that grows over the footpads.

To begin, gently but firmly grasp one of his feet. Push away stray hairs, and then position the clipper just over the tip of the nail. Close with a firm snap to cut the nail. Never trim more than an eighth of an inch (.25 cm) at a time. Be careful not to cut the *quick*, the sensitive area running the length of the nail that contains nerves and blood supply. The quick is difficult to see in dark-colored nails, so trim only the portion of the nail that curves downward. If the nail starts to bleed, apply styptic powder to the nail tip or use a nail cautery device to stop the flow. After you have clipped all the nails—and the dewclaws, if present—smooth the rough edges with an emery board. Be sure to trim the hair that grows over the footpads to prevent your Cairn from slipping on smooth floors.

Fleas and Ticks

During routine grooming, carefully examine your Cairn's skin. It should be healthy and clean, with no indication of irritation, flaking, or sores. If your dog is scratching more than usual—especially on the rump above the tail—he might have flea allergy dermatitis, a reaction to the saliva of biting fleas. However, you probably won't find parasites on your dog. Because fleas are remarkable jumpers, they spend most of their time off the dog, nestled in bedding material, carpets, and grass. Their calling card is the black specks of fecal matter they leave behind in the fur. Fleas not only produce acute itching, but also can transmit tapeworms and a variety of diseases. Although most infestations occur in warm, humid climates, fleas also exist in the arid regions of the

southwestern United States. Further, fleas can live in a warm house year-round.

Preventing and eliminating fleas may seem like a never-ending challenge to many pet owners. To win the battle, you must treat both your dog and his surroundings. Effective insecticides include shampoos, dips, powders, foams, and collars. Spot-on products, which contain insect-growth regulators, are applied to the skin between the shoulder blades. These kill adult fleas, as well as their eggs and larvae; ticks; and mosquitoes, depending on the formulation. In addition, a prescription medicine in the form of a once-a-month tablet given orally works when a female flea bites a treated dog and then passes the active ingredient into her eggs. By curbing a critical step in the reproductive process, flea eggs cannot develop, and the life cycle is broken.

Other parasites that feed on dogs include the American dog tick, brown dog tick, and black-legged or deer tick. Ticks can carry Rocky Mountain spotted fever, Lyme disease, and Ehrlichiosis, serious diseases that afflict both humans and dogs. Their bites also may cause skin irritation, sores, and occasionally tick paralysis. Dogs that spend much of their time outdoors pick up ticks in woods, tall grass, and shrubbery. However, birds, rodents, deer, and other small animals can bring them right into your backyard. Be sure to inspect your Cairn's coat and skin after a walk in woods or fields. If you find a tick, grasp it with tweezers as close to the skin as possible, and pull straight up with steady pressure. Then clean the area with rubbing alcohol. Spot-on products and collars aid in repelling ticks. Ask the veterinarian whether your Cairn needs a Lyme disease vaccination.

Dental Care

The buildup of tartar on your Cairn's teeth can lead to bad breath, sore gums, and—if untreated—tooth loss. When the pain becomes severe, dogs often become irritable and stop eating. Also, bacteria that form in the mouth can spread via the bloodstream to other areas of the body, where they contribute to heart and kidney disease, and other serious illnesses. Elderly pets, in particular, are susceptible to bacteria-related problems.

To accustom your new pet to having his teeth cleaned, begin gentle cleaning as soon as he comes home. Apply some doggie toothpaste to a toothbrush or piece of gauze, and rub it gently over the teeth and gums. For puppies, use a cat toothbrush that has bristles only at the tip. There are also several oral rinses on the market that fight tartar buildup.

However, despite the regular care you give at home, some animals have such a problem with tartar deposits that the veterinarian must remove them with special instruments and polishing agents. Dental scaling typically is performed under short-acting anesthesia. After a professional cleaning, the veterinarian may apply a sealant that prevents plaque-forming bacteria from attaching to the teeth. You may continue this protection at home with weekly applications of a prescription gel. To further guard against gum disease, ask about the *porphyromonas* dental vaccine that targets key bacteria responsible for plaque formation.

Ear Care

Another area that needs attention is the ears. Are they pink, healthy, and free of odor? Is there any waxy matter or discharge? If your Cairn is scratching his ears or shaking his head, he may have an infection or allergy. Infections often come from water in the ear canals, excess wax, or insect bites. Allergies result from substances in the environment, such as grasses, pollen, or dust mites, or even from the food your dog eats. To keep the ears free of waxy deposits, wipe the outer part of the canal with a cotton ball soaked in ear-cleaning solution. Don't probe inside the canal, especially with cotton swabs, because this can push waxy material deeper. Hair that grows inside the ear is left in place in the Cairn.

Hand Stripping

If you examine the outer coat, you'll notice that each hair varies in tone from root to tip, which gives the Cairn a brindled, or shaded, appearance. Clipping or cutting destroys the distinctive color, as well as the texture of the coat. When the dead hair is trimmed, but not removed, the coat becomes soft and loses its water-repellent characteristics. Dogs quickly become dirty when the undercoat is exposed, and some produce excessive dandruff. The best way to keep your Cairn in proper condition is to hand strip the outer coat every six to eight months.

Stripping removes the dead hair, which is ready to come out, and allows the emergence of new, even growth. Dogs that have been stripped also shed less and remain cleaner than clipped dogs, making them suitable for allergy-prone individuals.

Hand stripping is fairly simple when the coat is ready to come out. To begin, grasp a few strands between your fingers and pull steadily with the direction of growth. Gently stretch the skin as you release the hairs. Dead hair comes out easily—if you have to pull hard, the coat isn't yet ready to be stripped. To get a better grip on the hair shafts, apply grooming chalk to the coat or wear latex gloves. If you use a stripping knife, be careful not to cut or break the hairs instead of pulling them. A stripping stone (a small, square piece of lava) helps to remove the undercoat from the sensitive chest and belly areas. Finally, tidy the feet and backs of the ears with thinning shears.

Pet Grooming

Depending on your Cairn's age at the time of purchase, some grooming already may have been completed. Breeders usually neaten the appearance of the ears by removing stray hairs when puppies are about six weeks old. Many also remove the dark, or black, overlay of hairs that starts to loosen at 8 to 12 weeks. This not only gives an attractive look, but also allows the new adult coat to come in properly. The first major grooming, though, takes place when your puppy reaches 8 to 10 months. When the coat starts to "open" and part down the back, it must be completely removed. You may choose to have a professional handle this twice-yearly grooming, but make certain he or she has experi-

When the coat begins to look "blousy" and parts down the back, the long, dead strands must be removed by a process called plucking or stripping.

ence with terrier coats. If you decide to tackle the job yourself, complete the task within a few days so the new coat will be an even length. The Mars Coat-King is a favorite stripping tool of many owners. Just "brush" lightly in the direction of the hair growth to remove loose hair and undercoat. (Be careful not to strip too much.) Choose a coarse blade for the undercoat and a fine blade for finishing. The CTCA's grooming guidebook is highly recommended for all Cairn owners (see Information, page 91).

Rolling the Coat

Because show dogs must look their best for competitions that take place throughout the year, most handlers use a process called "rolling the coat" to keep their terriers in top form. This involves plucking all of the long, dead hairs on an ongoing basis, about every seven to ten days. Removing only a few hairs at a time and controlling the emergence of new coat ensures that show dogs are always presentable. Handlers also comb out the dead undercoat when it's ready to be shed. However, some Cairns don't have enough thickness or coarseness to permit rolling the coat. In that case, time the full-coat stripping to coincide with the dog's show schedule.

Grooming for the Show Ring

The technical skills and artistic aptitude necessary to present the Cairn Terrier in the show ring take many years, if not a lifetime, to master. Correct grooming not only enhances a dog's strengths, it also helps to disguise his faults.

Poor or excessive grooming can destroy the prospects of even a superior specimen. Because a casual appearance is an integral part of breed type, exhibitors must never show their Cairns in the highly stylized fashion of West Highland White Terriers or Scottish Terriers.

Although instruction in the finer points of show grooming is beyond the scope of this book, it's important for beginners to be able to visualize the relevant points of the standard, as well as the "perfect" Cairn, during grooming sessions. The breeder usually is the best source of information on proper technique. Briefly, show preparation involves a combination of rolling the coat and judicious trimming with thinning shears to blend different parts of the coat into each other. The Cairn must have no visible demarcation lines from one part of his body to another, but must possess a well-furnished cloak of medium-length hair.

Never use scissors or thinning shears to groom the head. The dead coat must be pulled by hand.

To keep your Cairn in peak condition, feed a well-balanced diet that is formulated for your dog's stage of development.

Food for Every Cairn

To keep your Cairn Terrier healthy and vigorous, it's important to select and feed a high-quality diet. The food must not only provide adequate nutrients for the various functions that take place within the body, but also be formulated for your pet's stage of development. In the past, dogs often consumed a diet based on table scraps and leftovers. Whether or not this offered sufficient nourishment was a hit-or-miss proposition, at best. Within the past several decades, though, breeders and veterinarians have joined forces to help define the nutritional requirements of dogs, and to create appropriate pet foods to meet those needs. Today, with more than 300 manufacturers annually producing 7 million tons of pet food, valued at $16 billion, selecting the correct formula challenges even experienced owners.

How, then, can you choose the best food for your Cairn? Puppies, as well as adults, need six kinds of nutrients: protein, carbohydrates, fat, vitamins, minerals, and water. The term *nutrient* refers to any factor that aids in the body's metabolic processes, such as regulating temperature, acting as structural components, or transporting substances throughout the bloodstream. However, depending on your dog's age, activity level, environment, and health status, the amount and balance of these nutrients will differ.

The Basic Nutrient Groups

Protein: Found in foods such as beef, chicken, eggs, grains, and soybeans, protein is essential for normal growth, muscle and bone formation, tissue repair, and internal body functions. Keratin, one type of protein, makes up the basic structure of skin, hair, and toenails. Collagen, another form, constitutes connective tissue, such as tendons, ligaments, and muscles. During digestion, protein is broken down into smaller substances called amino acids, which help to build as well as repair tissue. The body produces some of these, and the diet supplies others.

Most commercial foods use a combination of protein sources to ensure that they provide all the required amino acids. Puppies, active dogs, and nursing mothers need diets that contain between 25 and 30 percent protein. Deficiencies, particularly during growth, may cause skeletal disorders, weight loss, skin and hair problems, and lowered resistance to disease. Excesses, too, may be harmful, especially for senior dogs with reduced kidney function.

Carbohydrates: The carbohydrates from grain and vegetable sources provide your Cairn with energy. The sugar in carbohydrates is carried to the liver, where it's changed into glycogen and stored for later energy demands. Glucose plays a critical role in nourishing the brain because it's one of the few substances that can cross the blood-brain barrier. Dogs develop hypoglycemia when their blood sugar levels become too low, and if the condition is not treated promptly, they can go into shock and die. Carbohydrates also supply fiber, which plays a key role in the digestive process. Some forms are useful when dogs have diarrhea or constipation; others help to lower the level of cholesterol in the blood. Because fiber decreases the absorption of nutrients, puppies and active dogs should avoid diets high in roughage. If your dog is overweight, though, fiber allows him to feel full while it shortens the time food remains in the intestinal tract.

Dietary fat: Fat is a concentrated source of energy that is important during growth, high activity, pregnancy, or when nursing puppies. Fat also aids in the absorption of the fat-soluble vitamins, A, D, E, and K, and supplies the essential fatty acids, linoleic and linolenic acids. Dogs can develop fatty-acid deficiencies when they consume poor-quality dry foods or diets too low in fat. Signs include slow growth, reproductive difficulties, weight loss, flaky skin, and dull coat. (You can combat this problem by adding a teaspoon of vegetable oil to your dog's dinner, or by using one of the fatty-acid supplements on the market.) Too much fat also causes problems, including obesity, pancreatitis (inflammation of the pancreas), and steatorrhea (fat the dog cannot digest, passed in the stool). Dogs that consume high-fat diets usually eat less food, overall, so nutritional imbalances may occur as well.

Vitamins: Your dog needs organic compounds for healthy growth and development. Vitamins don't supply energy directly, but rather serve as coenzymes that help to regulate various processes within the body. Vitamins are classified into two groups—fat soluble or water soluble—according to the way they are absorbed, stored, and excreted.

Minerals: Less than 1 percent of your dog's weight, minerals serve a variety of necessary functions: They help to adjust the blood's acid-base balance, maintain the balance of water within the cells, and form the structural components of bones and teeth. Most pet foods supply adequate levels of minerals, so supplementation is usually unnecessary. The most important factor is the *balance* of minerals, especially calcium and phosphorus. Imbalances may lead to lameness, fractures, and abnormal bone development. When you choose a high-quality food, created for your dog's stage of life and activity level, you're providing a diet with the proper level and proportion of minerals.

Water: Your Cairn needs water more than any other nutrient. Although dogs can survive several days without food, a loss of only 10 to 15 percent of body water can lead to illness and even death. Dogs obtain water from drinking, as well as from the water content of their food and the metabolic processes that take place within the body. Because your pet's thirst response will increase or decrease depending on his diet, salt intake, exercise, weather, and temperament, be sure to provide plenty of fresh drinking water. Refill the bowl at least once a day. Your Cairn needs about two-and-a-half times as much water as the amount of dry matter in his dinner. Dogs usually regulate their water intake based on the outflow of fluids

Feeding Suggestions

- Choose a quiet, out-of-the-way place to feed your dog, and always feed him in the same place. Crate feeding may work well.
- Don't disturb your dog when he's eating.
- Don't serve food directly from the refrigerator or stove. Be careful of foods from the microwave; these may be too hot for your pet.
- Give your dog 15 to 20 minutes to eat, then remove any leftover dinner.
- If your dog leaves food, feed less next time. If your dog eats all his food and still looks hungry, add more at the next meal.
- Always provide fresh drinking water, but don't give your dog cold water; cool is best.
- Clean all bowls daily with hot water and soap.

from urination, panting, nursing puppies, or vomiting. However, if your Cairn begins to drink more or less than usual, consult the veterinarian.

Types of Dog Food

Dry food: Introduced in the late nineteenth century as an offshoot of the cereal industry, it's the most popular method of feeding. Most breeders use dry food, and you'll find a number of premium brands in this form. Advantages include convenience, ease of preparation and storage, cost, and easy cleanup. (Dogs that are fed dry food have smaller, firmer stools than do those that eat moist dog food.) Its low water content means you pay only for the food ingredients themselves, rather than fancy packaging. Most of the nutrients in dry food come from cereal grains, soybeans, vegetables, and meat

Daily Feeding Guidelines for a 10-Pound Dog

Food/Nutrient	Amount
Skinless chicken	2 oz. to 3 oz.
Brown rice	$1/2$ cup cooked
Peas and carrots	$1/4$ to $1/2$ cup cooked
Salt substitute (potassium chloride)	$1/8$ teaspoon
Vegetable oil	1 teaspoon
Calcium citrate	125 mg.
Daily multivitamin/mineral supplement	subject to label instructions

Information provided by Paula Terifaj, D.V.M., of Founders Veterinary Clinic (*www.foundersvet.com*).

or chicken meal. Manufacturers add extra fat, vitamins, and minerals to create a complete balanced diet. Dry food is especially good for the teeth because chewing helps to scrape off plaque and tartar. However, if you're feeding a young puppy, you may want to soften his food first by mixing it with warm water. Problems occur mainly in inexpensive brands, which may be difficult to digest or too low in nutrients. Always check the expiration date on the package. Products that use natural preservatives, such as vitamin E, have shorter shelf lives than those using the additives BHA, BHT, or ethoxyquin.

Canned food: Two forms of canned food are available: meat and ration varieties. Meat products consist mainly of meat and meat by-products, along with expanded nuggets of soy flour known as textured vegetable protein. Colored brown or red, these pieces are easy to mistake for meat chunks if you're unfamiliar with canned pet food. Most meat dinners also contain vitamins and minerals because the all-meat preparations of the past often led to serious nutritional imbalances. In fact, because it

contains more protein and fat than other products, canned meat should be given chiefly when your dog's energy needs are high—during growth, stress, pregnancy, or lactation. Small amounts may be added to dry food to improve its taste. Canned rations, on the other hand, offer a balance of meat, carbohydrates, dietary fat, vitamins, and minerals, and are suitable for all stages of life. A number of premium canned foods look and taste like human-grade stew, with an appealing mixture of meat and vegetables. Always store opened cans of food in the refrigerator, and don't leave uneaten food in your dog's bowl.

Soft-moist food: Shaped like hamburger patties or meat chunks, soft-moist products combine fresh meat with grains or soybeans, vitamins and minerals, fat, and water to form a flavorful, easy-to-digest diet. These foods are convenient to use, simple to store, and travel well. They are an ideal size for Cairns because most dogs need only one package per feeding. Soft-moist foods also don't require refrigeration. However, manufacturers usually add preservatives and humectants to prevent the products from spoiling and drying out. Dogs with allergies may not tolerate these additives, some of which include sugar or food coloring, and may develop diarrhea or vomiting. Make certain the cellophane is intact because contact with air can cause the food to become rancid.

Home cooking: This method is growing in popularity, particularly since the 2007 recall of more than 150 brands of contaminated pet food that sickened or killed dogs and cats. To ensure that your Cairn receives the proper balance of nutrients, it's important to select from a variety of ingredients. Quality protein sources include beef, poultry, fish, eggs, and dairy products (if tolerated). Organ meat, such as liver or kidney, may be added in small amounts. Suitable vegetables, such as broccoli, squash, peas, carrots, green beans, and sweet potato, provide carbohydrates for energy, as well as vitamins and minerals. Grains also play a role by adding fiber to improve digestion. Most home-cooked diets also need to be supplemented with vitamins and minerals—especially calcium. If you're willing to make the commitment in time, energy, and added costs to cook for your Cairn, be sure to obtain a scientifically based guidebook and follow the recipes exactly. The veterinarian also may recommend a diet that provides complete and balanced nutrition.

Raw feeding: In their quest to improve the health and longevity of their pets, many owners have adopted a diet based on raw foods. One popular plan goes by the acronym BARF, which stands for "Bones and Raw Food" or "Biologically Appropriate Raw Food." The premise behind this method is that an "evolutionary" diet offers greater health benefits than do cooked foods. Advocates believe that high temperatures used

A dog's nutritional status is often reflected in the health of his skin and coat. This Cairn's thick and lustrous fur is a result of eating a well-balanced diet.

in processing destroy vital nutrients and enzymes. Three raw-feeding methods are available: fully homemade meals, grain products to which raw meat is added, and packaged frozen foods that need no further supplementation. By feeding the type of diet consumed by the dog's wild ancestors—based on raw muscle meat, organs, meaty bones, vegetables, and fruit— supporters suggest that pets can enjoy fresher breath with fewer dental problems, better coats and less odor, and improved immune function. However, the American Veterinary Medical Association and practicing veterinarians have raised concerns about the possible presence of bacteria, such as E. coli and salmonella, and parasites in raw meat. Also, consuming raw bones may lead to fractured teeth and intestinal perforations or blockages that require emergency surgery. Few scientific studies have been performed, to date, to verify the health claims of raw food enthusiasts.

Probiotics: Breeders who have practiced adding a dollop of yogurt—which contains live cultures of "friendly" bacteria—to their dogs' diets may be on to something. *Probiotics*, as these living beneficial microbes are called, reside in the gastrointestinal tract, where they compete against other, more harmful, organisms. Changes in diet, stress, and using antibiotics or other prescription medications may alter this balance. When harmful bacteria take over, dogs often develop diarrhea, constipation, vomiting, or food allergies. Probiotics not only decrease these problems, but also confer a variety of health benefits. They guard against infections and allergies, support the immune system, and may even reduce the risk of developing cancer. Probiotics also produce vitamins, such as biotin and folic acid, and complete the digestion of certain nutrients.

If your Cairn's balance of healthy versus harmful bacteria has been compromised, consider adding probiotics to his diet in the form of tablets or powder sprinkled on his food. Choose a broad-spectrum product that contains more than one strain. (No single form helps every problem.) It may take 10 to 14 days for probiotics to colonize the GI tract. Always choose a high-quality supplement. Keep in mind that probiotics are living microbes, which may be killed by excessive heat or moisture, so store them in the refrigerator.

Prescription diets: Because the food your dog eats plays a critical role in the management and treatment of certain diseases, researchers and manufacturers have developed an assortment of special diets, available by prescription from the veterinarian. For example, dogs with acute kidney disease maintain or improve their condition on meals with lower levels of protein. Dogs with heart failure require reduced-sodium foods. Because these scientifically formulated diets come in convenient dry or canned recipes, you can take a significant step in improving your dog's health with a minimum of effort.

Feeding Your Cairn Terrier

You'll need to regulate the amount of food your dog eats, depending on his or her activity level, age, and stage of life. Generally, Cairns need 30 to 35 calories per pound of body weight, or about one half to two thirds of a cup of high-quality dry food each day. If your dog is active, involved in a rigorous schedule of competitions, pregnant, or nursing puppies, he or she needs more food than average. Dogs that are inactive or overweight require less. Use the feeding recommendations on the package only as a guideline. Your Cairn's physical condition is the ultimate test in deciding how much to feed. Ideally, you should be able to feel a thin layer of flesh (not fat) covering the ribs, and the hip bones should not be sharp or prominent to your

Types of Probiotics
- Lactobacillus
- Bifidobacterium
- Escherichia
- Enterococcus
- Saccharomyces (yeast)

touch. By weighing your dog periodically, you can note any changes and adjust your feeding program accordingly.

Special Nutritional Needs

Puppies

When you purchase your new puppy, one of the supplies you should receive from the breeder is a small amount of the food he has been eating, along with instructions on when and how much to feed. Your Cairn will grow rapidly in his first year, from a bouncing pup to a dignified adult. To make certain he receives the nutrients he needs, choose a food made especially for puppies. It should be energy dense, easy to digest, and at least 29 percent protein. Be sure the label guarantees the food is complete and balanced. Your puppy will need a smaller amount of food, overall, if you feed a high-quality brand.

Adult Dogs

When your Cairn approaches his first birthday, you may notice he has begun to reduce his activity level, along with his food intake. This is the time to change your dog's diet to a maintenance formula. Whenever you make a feeding change, introduce the new food gradually to avoid causing digestive upsets. Start by mixing one quarter of the adult food with three quarters of the puppy food. Continue to add more of the new dinner until your dog is eating it exclusively. Be sure to have a bowl of water available.

Active Dogs

Few Cairns work for a living as did their ancestors. However, your dog may expend nearly as much energy when he competes on the show circuit, trains for and performs in Obedience trials, or simply plays in the backyard. Canned and dry performance foods, with their higher levels of nutrients and easy-to-

These active Cairns require greater amounts of nutrients than do sedentary or senior pets.

digest formulas, work well for dogs under both emotional and physical stress. Another way to increase the energy content of the diet is to add one-half to one tablespoon of vegetable oil to your dog's regular dry dinner.

The most important nutrient your dog needs when he's active is water. Dogs don't perspire, but they lose fluid when they pant. Always provide water during and after exercise, competition, or travel.

Overweight Dogs

Although Cairns are active and alert little dogs, they have a tendency to gain weight. In fact, a study done in the United Kingdom indicated that Cairn Terriers were the second most likely breed to become obese, after Labrador Retrievers. This may be due to hereditary factors or their hearty appetites. Other causes may include lack of exercise, boredom, and age. Excess weight contributes to heart, liver, and kidney disease; cancer; skin problems; arthritis; and reproductive difficulties. Overweight dogs face greater risks during surgery, both from the procedure itself and the anesthesia. Obesity affects not only the quality of your dog's life, but also his life span. If your Cairn needs to lose weight, have the veterinarian perform a thorough checkup. Certain illnesses can cause weight gain, and fluid retention, parasites, and pregnancy sometimes are mistaken for excess weight.

The best way to help your dog lose weight is to combine exercise with a high-fiber, reduced-calorie food designed for overweight dogs. Unless the veterinarian has uncovered a condition that activity could worsen, take your Cairn for one or two 15- to 20-minute walks each day. Exercise helps to burn calories directly and

Foods to Avoid

Food	Active Component	Reactions
Avocado (leaves, fruit, bark, seeds)	Persin	Vomiting, pancreatitis, fluid buildup, breathing problems
Chocolate (from most to least toxic: cacao beans, cocoa powder, baking chocolate, dark and semisweet chocolate, milk and white chocolate)	Theobromine, caffeine	Vomiting, diarrhea, restlessness, panting, excessive thirst and urination, seizures, fast or irregular heartbeat, coma, death
Grapes and Raisins	Unknown	Acute kidney failure, death
Macadamia Nuts	Unknown	Muscle tremor, weakness, paralysis, pain, swelling, and stiffness in limbs
Onions and Garlic	Thiosulphate	Vomiting, diarrhea, breathing problems, hemolytic anemia
Tomatoes (leaves and stems, green tomatoes)	Tomatine, atropine	Vomiting, diarrhea, breathing problems, muscle tremor, weakness, paralysis, irregular heartbeat, coma, death

Other foods to avoid include artificial sweeteners, coffee and tea, fruit seeds and pits, raw fish, raw liver, raw egg whites, nutmeg, yeast dough, potatoes (green sprouts and green skin), and wild mushrooms.

continues to raise your dog's metabolism during rest. It also improves heart function and prevents the loss of muscle that often accompanies dieting. A daily walk provides a time you and your dog can be together, away from the distractions of a busy household, sharing the pleasure of each other's company.

Senior Dogs

When your Cairn reaches about eight years of age, consider switching his diet to a formula for senior dogs. Many complex processes take place during aging, including digestive changes, skin and coat problems, bone and joint disorders, and reduced organ function. Older dogs are frequently more sedentary than they once were and tend to put on weight. A few eat less because of dental problems, or changes in their senses of taste and smell. (Feeding canned food or adding warm water to dry food can help this.) Although some older dogs may need reduced levels of protein, phosphorus, sodium, and vitamin D, others require more protein, essential fatty acids, and vitamins A, B-complex, and E.

THE FUNDAMENTALS OF HEALTH CARE

A good breeder prepares for the health of a litter—even before the puppies are born—by screening the sire and dam for hereditary illnesses that could be passed to the next generation. To prevent your Cairn from developing future problems, provide a nutritious diet, adequate exercise and rest, and regular checkups by the veterinarian.

Locating a Veterinarian

Whether you're a first-time puppy owner or a veteran of the dog fancy, you'll probably have many questions about the well-being of the little Cairn Terrier entrusted to your care. Because the veterinarian is an important partner in keeping your dog healthy, be sure to choose one before you bring your new pet home. The breeder may suggest a veterinarian, if you're buying locally. Other recommendations may come from dog-owning friends or neighbors, groomers, boarding kennels, or

Don't allow your Cairn to exercise in areas that have been treated with insecticides, herbicides, or various lawn chemicals until at least several rainstorms have made the products harmless. Such compounds have been known to cause seizures, which sometimes last throughout the dog's lifetime.

veterinary associations. Also, check the yellow pages for animal clinics near your home.

After you've narrowed your choices to two or three, make an appointment to talk with the doctors and, if possible, tour the areas of the buildings that are open to the public. Observe the hospital environment as well as the staff members. Is this the kind of place you would want to bring your Cairn? Is the building clean, bright, and relatively free of unpleasant odors? Are the receptionist's duties handled efficiently? Do all employees seem to genuinely care about pets? Are the location and hours convenient? Take your time and don't be afraid to ask questions. Your pet's health depends on the care he receives now and throughout his lifetime.

The First Examination

When you purchase your Cairn from a reputable breeder, you're choosing a puppy with the belief that he's healthy and free of apparent defects. Many breeders provide a guarantee that offers a refund or replacement if a problem is found. It's necessary, therefore, to have your Cairn examined as soon as possible—within 48 to 72 hours. During this visit, the veterinarian will listen to the heart and lungs, inspect the coat and skin, feel for any swellings, go over the legs and joints, and check the eyes, ears, and teeth. Be sure to take any records of prior vaccinations, and bring a fresh stool sample so the technician can test for worms or their eggs. Ask any questions you might have about your Cairn. You'll find it helpful, especially as your pet ages, to keep a record of all exams, noting symptoms, prescribed medications, shots, surgeries, and other procedures. A comprehensive home veterinary manual is a must for all owners.

Preventive Care

Vaccinations: Puppies receive temporary immunity to certain infectious diseases at birth from antibodies, or special protein molecules, in their mother's milk. However, this protection lasts only a few weeks. By the time puppies are about six weeks old, they must develop their own immune systems. Dogs, like humans, form disease-fighting antibodies after exposure to mild or altered forms of antigens. The antibodies then travel throughout the bloodstream, ready to mount an attack if bacteria or viral organisms invade the body. Although a small degree of risk is present in any veterinary procedure, the safest way to expose dogs to these antigens is by a series of controlled vaccinations.

Your puppy will need inoculations every two or three weeks until about 16 to 20 weeks of age. Depending on the diseases that are present where you live, the vaccines may include antigens for distemper, parvovirus, parainfluenza, hepatitis, adenovirus, and rabies. Remember, until he is fully vaccinated, your Cairn is at risk of contracting an infectious illness. Avoid taking your puppy to parks, dog shows, or other places where strange animals gather. After your Cairn reaches adulthood, it's important to schedule regular booster shots to keep his immune system strong.

Heartworms are responsible for serious illness—even death—in dogs. Transmitted by a bite from an infected mosquito, rather than by dog-to-dog contact, the parasites are found throughout the United States and Canada. Heartworms live in the heart, lungs, and large blood vessels, where they can grow 4 to 12 inches long. Because adult worms often live for several years within a dog's body, they produce thousands of microscopic worms. When a mosquito bites a dog that has circulating microfilaria, the mosquito becomes infected and can transmit the worms to another dog. Both adult and immature heartworms may exist in a dog for years without signs of disease. By the time owners notice coughing, difficulty breathing, or other problems, their pets are seriously ill. Treatment, which is aimed at killing adult as well as microscopic worms, has many potential complications.

Fortunately, heartworms can be prevented with medication. However, dogs that have never taken medication should be tested before they begin the first dose. One kind of test, in which a blood sample is examined under a microscope, shows microfilaria circulating in the bloodstream. This suggests the presence of adult worms, but doesn't discern them directly. A more sensitive test finds a specific antigen produced in the presence of adult female heartworms. A recently developed antibody test can detect even a single male heartworm. Testing should be done annually, before your dog starts the next season's medication. The best age to begin heartworm prevention, especially if you live in a region with a heavy mosquito infestation, is between 9 and 12 weeks. Your Cairn safely can take a once-a-month pill or chewable tablet, or a daily chewable. These may be used year-round or for the duration of mosquito season. Some preventives also help to combat hookworms, roundworms, and whipworms.

Neutering: The most important step you can take to ensure your Cairn's health—next to obtaining yearly vaccinations—is to neuter your puppy before he reaches sexual maturity. The surgical procedure in which the sex organs are removed is called spaying in females and castrating in males. Neutering not only avoids the possibility that a dog will become accidentally pregnant or sire an unwanted litter, but also offers numerous benefits to the dog's physical and emotional well-being. For example, spaying before six months of age nearly eliminates the chances that a female will contract mammary, uterine, or ovarian cancers. It also avoids the problems associated with twice-yearly heat cycles. The hormonal changes that take place during these seasons may be one of the risk factors for developing reproductive cancers.

Males, too, benefit from early castration. They are less likely to show undesirable behaviors, such as marking their territory or roaming. Castration also helps to reduce the possibility of developing testicular cancer, prostate disease, hormonal dysfunction, and perianal adenoma, a growth around the anus. Although

neutering is major surgery, it's considered safe—especially for young dogs with immature reproductive organs. (Neutered dogs cannot compete in the show ring, but may participate in all Obedience and Performance events.)

Basic Procedures

Checking the Pulse Rate

To count your Cairn's heartbeat, place your hand directly over his heart, on the left side of the chest behind the elbow. You also can take the pulse at the femoral artery, located at the inner part of the thigh. In healthy dogs, the pulse is strong and steady. A normal rate may be up to 180 beats per minute in puppies, and 60 to 160 in adults. A rapid or slow pulse can signal different ailments, so always bring changes in the heart rate to the veterinarian's attention.

Collecting Fecal and Urine Samples

If your dog is sick, you may need to collect fecal or urine samples to locate parasites or determine the cause of an infection. By viewing the samples under a microscope, the doctor is able to prescribe the best medication, as well as monitor the treatment process. If your pet has an infection or shows signs of kidney disease, you may need to collect samples throughout the course of the illness. To obtain a urine sample, place a small disposable container under your dog when he urinates. Then, transfer it to a clean bottle. Always collect urine in the morning when it's more concentrated. Fecal specimens should be examined within three hours of obtaining them, especially if the veterinarian must check for parasite eggs. When eggs mature and burst, they become more difficult to identify.

Giving Medication

To give your dog a pill, grasp the top of his muzzle behind the canine teeth and gently press the lips inward until he opens his mouth. With your other hand, place the tablet as far back on the tongue as possible. Close your dog's mouth, tilt his head back, and stroke his throat until he swallows. If your pet has difficulty taking pills, place them in small treats. A pill may be concealed in a bit of cheese, meat, or peanut butter and offered to the Cairn. If your dog is used to treats he will generally swallow the medication easily. Check to make certain the pill has not been rejected while the treat is consumed. Some medications are specially coated, time-release formulas, so never crush a pill without checking with the doctor. To give liquid medicine, use a plastic eyedropper marked with a measuring scale. Form a pocket between your dog's cheek and teeth by gently pulling the skin outward. Hold his head upright and slowly squeeze a small amount of liquid into the pocket. Stroke his throat until he swallows. Never pour liquids directly down the throat because your pet could choke or inhale the fluid.

Taking Temperature

Lubricate a rectal thermometer with petroleum jelly and insert the bulb about an inch into your dog's rectum. Hold it in place for the recommended length of time, depending on the kind of thermometer you're using. If you have difficulty with a rectal thermometer, try an ear thermometer that measures the infrared heatwaves from the eardrum.

Normal body temperature is between 100.5° and 102.5°F. Slight variations may be due to excitement or exercise, but a reading higher than 102.5°F usually indicates a fever.

Common Ailments

Anal Sac Problems

Located on the lower left and right sides of the anus are two anal sacs. Although their exact purpose is unknown, the secretion they produce may lubricate the rectum and allow dogs to pass their bowel movements more eas-

ily. The distinctive scent from the sacs also might help animals determine the sex of others during greeting rituals. Sometimes the sacs don't empty fully and become impacted with material. When this happens, you may notice your Cairn is scooting across the floor, and you may smell a strong, unpleasant odor. The veterinarian can express the fluid by gently pressing the sacs. If the sacs become infected, they can swell and rupture through the skin. These abscesses usually respond to antibiotics, warm compresses, and low doses of aspirin.

Constipation

Dogs normally have a bowel movement after each meal. However, if your pet routinely has fewer movements, it's no cause for concern. Dogs with constipation usually strain or feel pain when they attempt to have a movement. Constipation may occur if your Cairn eats a low-fiber dinner, or when he overeats. It also results from eating indigestible material, such as grass, paper, or cloth. Never give your dog natural bones because they can splinter and cause fecal impaction. For occasional bouts of constipation, give milk of magnesia or add a teaspoon of mineral oil to your dog's dinner. Change to a food with more fiber, and make certain your Cairn gets plenty of exercise. If constipation persists, contact the veterinarian.

Diarrhea

This is a common complaint in all breeds, partly due to the dog's short colon, which has difficulty absorbing all the fluid from undigested food in the intestines. Changes in diet, infections, worms, allergies, and stress also can cause diarrhea. For mild cases, withhold food for 12 to 24 hours, but provide ice cubes for water.

Give one-half to one teaspoon of liquid anti-diarrhea medication every four to six hours. Follow with a bland diet of lean hamburger, cottage cheese, cooked egg, or rice. Adding a tablespoon of plain canned pumpkin (not pie filling) to the dinner helps both constipation and diarrhea. If you notice vomiting, fever, or blood in the feces, or diarrhea lasts longer than 36 hours, consult the veterinarian.

Worms

Those that affect dogs include roundworms, tapeworms, hookworms, and whipworms. Dogs can acquire worms in the uterus or through nursing from an infected mother, or from contact with contaminated soil or feces. Worms also may enter the body as a result of eating raw meat or fish. Fleas play a role in the spread of tapeworms, serving as the intermediate hosts. Pets usually get worms by sniffing or licking infected material. However, the larval stage of hookworms can penetrate the skin.

Because puppies may be born with worms, their stools should be examined at two to three weeks of age and again at five to six weeks. Be sure to bring a fresh stool sample to the first veterinary appointment. To prescribe the best medication, if it's needed, the veterinarian must examine the specimen under a microscope to identify the kind of worm involved. He or she then can choose the safest product to use. When your pet is rid of worms, you can help to prevent reinfestation by keeping your yard clean and free of feces. Also, avoid places where strange dogs come together. Worms are less of a problem in adult dogs, because they seem to acquire some natural immunity that helps them fight off the parasites. Medication given for heartworms offers protection against other types of worms as well.

Vomiting

Cairns may vomit as a result of excitement, nervousness, motion sickness, worms, or overeating. Several serious diseases also may cause vomiting. If your dog vomits, but seems normal with no other signs of illness, the condition probably is not serious. Withhold food for 12 to 24 hours, but provide ice cubes for water. Feed a bland diet for a day or two, and allow plenty of rest. If your pet has a fever or diarrhea, vomits blood or has blood in the stool, indicates pain, or is sick for more than 24 hours, contact the veterinarian.

Health Problems

Cairn Terriers are vigorous, long-lived dogs that usually remain active through their distinguished senior years. In fact, a life span of 14 to 17 years is common. However, breeders, owners, and veterinarians have identified several health problems that are significant to anyone considering the addition of a Cairn to the household. Some of these are hereditary (passed from one generation to another through the genes) or congenital (present at birth). Others occur as a result of nonspecific factors, such as infections, exposure to environmental toxins, injuries, or advancing age. The Cairn Terrier Club of America and the Cairn Terrier Health Watch, in the United Kingdom, have conducted studies that have uncovered the presence of the conditions listed below. The Canine Eye Registration Foundation (CERF) and the Orthopedic Foundation for Animals (OFA) maintain registries for diseases that affect Cairns. To help reduce the occurrence of hereditary diseases in their bloodlines, breeders voluntarily submit their dogs' test results for research purposes, as well as for use by individuals who seek to make sound breeding decisions.

Eye Problems

Cataracts: One of the most common eye disorders among dogs, cataracts develop as a result of diabetes, injuries, or hereditary factors. When the lens becomes cloudy or opaque, light can no longer reach the retina at the back of the eye and vision becomes cloudy or blurred. If the cataract continues to grow unchecked, dogs may lose their sight altogether. Because pets readily adapt to changes in vision, especially in familiar surroundings, owners may not notice the onset of cataracts until the veterinarian discovers them during a routine examination. The most successful way to treat cataracts is to surgically remove the lens and replace it with an artificial lens. Healing usually is complete within a few weeks and most dogs experience a marked improvement in vision.

The Canine Eye Registration Foundation and the Orthopedic Foundation for Animals currently accept test results for the following hereditary diseases:

- Cataracts
- Entropion
- Progressive retinal atrophy
- Retinal dysplasia
- Corneal dystrophy
- Globoid cell leukodystrophy (Krabbe's disease)
- Hip and elbow dysplasia
- Legg-Calvé-Perthes disease
- Luxated patellas, elbows, and shoulders
- Thyroid disease
- Heart disease (congenital)

Glaucoma: This is a serious disease that can cause pain, blindness, and even loss of the eye if not treated promptly. Normally, the eye produces fluid that drains slowly from an opening at its front—the meeting point of the cornea and iris. Anything that interferes with this inflow or outflow results in a buildup of pressure within the eye. This prevents blood from reaching the retina, causing permanent damage to the optic nerve. Cairns have been found to have a specific form of secondary glaucoma, called **ocular melanosis** or **melanocytic glaucoma**, in which the iris thickens and tiny spots of pigment develop and accumulate in the cornea. Eventually, these spots block the drainage passageways, causing pressure and nerve destruction. Cairns between 9 and 13 years of age are typically affected, and most dogs are already blind when diagnosed.

Another problem that can lead to glaucoma—especially in certain terrier breeds—is **lens luxation**. Located behind the iris, the lens is held in place by suspensory ligaments. When the fibers become weakened or break, the lens can slip from its normal position (subluxation) or become totally detached (luxation). Some forms of luxation block the outflow of fluid, whereas others cause damage to the cornea.

Signs of glaucoma, which usually appear after the disease has progressed, include teariness, abnormal discharge, reddened eyes, sensitivity to light, and pain reactions such as withdrawal or loss of appetite. Ultimately, the pupil may become fixed and dilated (large), and the eyeball may swell in size. Medication doesn't have the success rate in dogs that it

does in humans, but eye drops and pills that reduce inner eye pressure and keep the pupil relatively constricted help some animals with mild glaucoma. Surgery to destroy the fluid-producing cells in the eye may save vision.

Another eye disease that affects Cairns—and more than 100 breeds worldwide—is **progressive retinal atrophy** (PRA). This condition, usually inherited recessively, causes degeneration of the retina. In healthy dogs, the retina is the area at the back of the eye that takes in light. Specialized photoreceptors, called rods and cones, line the retina and convert the incoming light into electrical impulses that travel along the optic nerve to the brain. There, the signals are interpreted as images. Rods are responsible for black-and-white and night vision, and cones enable color and day vision. Usually, rods lose their functional ability before cones, leading to the classic symptom of night blindness. PRA affects both photoreceptors in Cairns, with the age of onset less than one year. The breed also is susceptible to a condition called **retinal dysplasia**, or the malformation of the retina.

There are no outward signs of PRA, such as watery or red eyes. However, owners may notice dilated pupils and a shininess of the eye caused by the increased reflectivity of the tapetum behind the retina. PRA usually affects both eyes. Late in the disease, the lens may become cloudy or opaque and cataracts may form. Although there is no treatment for PRA, dogs rarely experience discomfort and usually adapt to their environments if given a little extra care by their owners.

A DNA test is available that identifies normal and affected dogs, as well as those that carry the gene mutation. An important resource for owners interested in learning more about hereditary eye diseases is the Canine Eye Registration Foundation (CERF) at Purdue University. (See Information, page 92.)

Neurological Disorders

Globoid cell leukodystrophy (GCL), or **Krabbe's Disease**, is a rare illness of the nervous system that infrequently occurs in Cairn puppies, as well as West Highland White Terriers and several other breeds. Beginning as early as four weeks of age, GCL is a degenerative disease of the white matter of the brain and spinal cord—and sometimes the peripheral nerves— that comes from a deficiency of a specific enzyme involved in lipid metabolism. Because GCL attacks the central nervous system, signs include weakness, loss of coordination, stum-

bling, tremor, blindness, and paralysis. There is no treatment for this recessively transmitted disease and affected puppies usually die by five or six months. A significant advance in eliminating GCL from bloodlines now exists with the development of a DNA-based blood test that can identify dogs that carry the defective gene.

The most common neurological problem, found in up to 5 percent of dogs, is the group of seizure disorders called **epilepsy**. Seizures take place due to the rapid, uncontrolled discharges of nerve cells. In Cairns, epilepsy usually begins by one or two years of age. Treatment, the success of which depends on the severity of the disease and its underlying causes (infection,

tumor, cancer, head injuries), involves giving the anti-seizure drug, phenobarbital or primidone, or a combination of medications. The gene involved in two rare forms of epilepsy was discovered in 2005, and researchers hope further investigation will locate the mutation involved in more common types of seizures.

Cardiovascular Disorders

Hemophilia A and **B** and **von Willebrand's Disease** (vWD), a group of blood clotting disorders, have been identified in a number of breeds. Transmitted as a sex-linked recessive trait, meaning the defective gene is carried by females but the disease appears mainly in males, hemophilia results from deficiencies in coagulation factors that allow the blood to clot properly. Von Willebrand's disease, which may be inherited from one or both parents depending on the form, comes from a decrease in a blood protein necessary for platelet function. Both cause abnormal bleeding, which first may be noticed during dewclaw removal or a routine surgical procedure. Other signs include unexplained bleeding from the nose or mouth, blood in the urine or feces, bruising, and swollen joints. Dogs with vWD should be tested for an underactive thyroid and treated, if necessary, with thyroid supplements. Some dogs with hemophilia or vWD also may need blood transfusions to replace missing clotting factors. Five genetic mutations have been identified in the inheritance of von Willebrand's disease, and DNA tests can detect normal and affected dogs, and carriers, in several breeds.

An uncommon problem of the cardiovascular system, usually found in puppies between 6 weeks and 12 months of age, is **portosystemic shunt**. Caused by a congenital defect that pre-vents the blood supply of the abdominal organs from reaching the liver, where toxins are removed, the disease mimics the signs of liver failure: abnormal behavior or seizures, lack of coordination, and overall poor health. Surgical correction is the most successful treatment when veterinarians discover the problem early enough.

Skeletal Disorders

An abnormality that causes the lower jaw and other bones in the skull to become roughened, dense, and hard, **craniomandibular osteopathy** (CMO), or "lion jaw," affects Cairns, Westies, and several other breeds. Signs, which begin in puppies from 4 to 8 months of age, include jaw swelling, pain during chewing, and sensitivity when the mouth is handled. Feeding softened foods and giving pain and anti-inflammatory medication help to reduce this discomfort. Fortunately, most dogs fully recover by two or three years. Because the disease is transmitted as a single recessive gene, carried by both parents, research is under way to locate a genetic marker for CMO.

Luxating patellas, or slipping kneecaps of the hind legs, are a common orthopedic problem in small dogs. Caused by weakness in the ligaments that support the kneecap, poor alignment of muscles and tendons, or a too-shallow groove in the femur, signs of patellar luxation include sudden limping, chronic lameness, or difficulty straightening the knee, usually accompanied by pain. Veterinarians can diagnose the disorder by manual examination of the kneecap, and by radiographs. Treatment involves rest, controlled exercise on leash, pain medication, and weight reduction, if needed. Surgery to deepen the femoral groove has been

quite successful, especially in young dogs or those with persistent lameness.

The canine hip is a ball-and-socket joint in which the muscles and ligaments, as well as the shape and fit of the ball (femoral head) within the socket (acetabulum), maintain stability yet provide a full range of motion. **Hip dysplasia** (HD), mainly observed in large breeds, and **Legg-Calvé-Perthes disease** (LCPD), seen in small breeds, occur in Cairn Terriers. Dogs with HD usually are born with normal-looking hips that later undergo structural changes. Loose ligaments, inadequate muscle tone, and shallow sockets are significant factors in developing the problem. LCPD, on the other hand, results from an interruption in the blood supply to the head of the femur. When vital nutrients cannot reach the area, bone cells die and the ball becomes flattened and distorted. Signs of both disorders include lameness, gait abnormalities, muscle wasting, and pain. Surgery

often is necessary to alleviate symptoms of both hip dysplasia and LCPD.

For more information about skeletal disorders in dogs, contact the Orthopedic Foundation for Animals (OFA), a nonprofit registry organization founded in 1966. (See Information, page 92.)

Other Problems

Conditions with a strong hereditary basis that also are found in Cairns include **cleft palate**, in which the palate fails to fully fuse before birth; **cryptorchidism**, one or both testicles retained within the abdomen; **atopic dermatitis**, allergic skin diseases; **cystinuria**, excessive excretion of the amino acid, cystine, in the urine; **hypothyroidism**, abnormally low production of thyroid hormones; and **inguinal hernia**, protrusion of an organ or tissue through a break in the muscular wall that occurs where the rear leg joins the body.

First aid is an emergency procedure administered to save your Cairn's life and prevent additional injury. It should never take the place of prompt veterinary attention. In case of serious accident or illness, remain calm and give priority to life-threatening conditions. Begin artificial respiration or heart massage, if needed. Control profuse bleeding before you attend to minor injuries.

Artificial Respiration

A dog can stop breathing for many reasons. Food, fluid, or a piece of toy or bone may block his air passages. Shock, injury, heart failure, and asphyxiation also can cause difficulty breathing. This is always a life-threatening emergency. Animals can die within three to five minutes after the oxygen supply has stopped. Make certain your

Correct position for mouth-to-nose artificial respiration.

dog's air passages are clear before you treat other injuries.

Manual Artificial Respiration:

- Place your dog on his side, extending the head and neck to straighten the airway.
- Open the mouth and pull the tongue forward. Remove any matter inside the mouth.
- Place both hands on the chest, between the shoulder blades and last rib.
- Press firmly for two to three seconds.
- Release the pressure for two to three seconds.
- Repeat until your dog breathes on his own.

Mouth-to-Nose Artificial Respiration (if the chest has been injured):

- Pull your dog's tongue forward and close the mouth.
- Blow into the nostrils until the lungs expand.
- Remove your mouth so that air is expelled.
- Repeat until your dog breathes on his own.

Bleeding

Severe bleeding is an emergency that requires immediate action. Always control bleeding before you treat minor injuries. Keep your dog quiet and apply a sterile gauze pad or clean

cloth to the wound. Press firmly until the bleeding stops. If you need to use a second gauze pad, place it directly over the original dressing without removing the first bandage. If this fails to control the bleeding, make a tourniquet from strips of gauze or cloth. Wrap around the injured limb above the wound (between the wound and the heart) and tie a half-knot. Place a pencil on top of the loop and knot. Tighten carefully to stop bleeding. *Tourniquets must be used with extreme caution to avoid cutting off the circulation to the affected area.* Be sure to seek immediate veterinary assistance. Many animal hospitals have supplies of canine blood products on hand, and can give transfusions in cases of extreme blood loss.

Choking

Symptoms of choking include gasping for breath, gagging, pawing at the mouth or throat, and salivation. If your dog is deprived of oxygen, he can lose consciousness and die within minutes. A procedure similar to the Heimlich maneuver used for humans is often successful in dislodging food or a foreign object blocking your dog's airway.

Heimlich-like Maneuver

- Open your dog's mouth and pull the tongue forward. See if you can reach the obstruction with your fingers or forceps.
- Place your dog on his side. Using both hands, press the abdomen below the rib cage with a firm upward thrust.
- Repeat until your dog expels the foreign object, or you can extract it with forceps.
- Give artificial respiration if breathing has stopped, and contact the veterinarian.

Fractures

Dogs can break their legs when they jump from a high surface, slip on snow or ice, or run loose and get hit by a car. Signs of a fracture include limping, crying out in pain, swelling at the site, or exposed bone. First, treat for bleeding or shock; then, pad the limb with a temporary splint. Wrap gently with gauze or cloth strips. Place splints on the top and bottom of the fracture and tie in place. You may need to muzzle a dog that snaps as a reaction to pain. Seek prompt veterinary assistance.

Cardiac Arrest

Your dog's heart may stop beating as a result of injury, poisoning, electrical shock (chewing an appliance cord), or serious illness. If you cannot detect a heartbeat, begin heart massage at once. You also may need to provide artificial respiration.

Heart Massage

- Loosen your dog's collar and check the airway for obstruction.
- Lay your dog on his right side. Place the palms of both hands on the top and bottom of the chest. (For puppies, place the thumb on one side of the chest and the fingers on the other.)
- Push downward with the hand on top, using the bottom hand for support. Repeat compression six times, then wait five seconds. (For artificial respiration, give two to three breaths.)
- Continue heart massage until the heart begins to beat on its own, or you cannot detect a pulse. A dog can live only three to four minutes after his heart has stopped beating.

Heat Exhaustion and Heat Stroke

Dogs don't perspire through their pores. Because they release body heat mainly through panting, they cannot tolerate prolonged exposure to heat. The most common causes of heat-strokes are leaving a dog in a closed car, kenneling outdoors without enough shade or water, and exercising in hot weather. Puppies, elderly or overweight dogs, and those with chronic health problems are most susceptible to heat exhaustion or heat stroke. Symptoms include elevated body temperature, rapid heartbeat, staggering, dilated pupils, and pale gums. Cool your dog immediately with cold compresses or ice packs, or soak him in cool water. Monitor his body temperature to ensure it doesn't fall below normal.

Correct demonstration of heart massage.

ACTIVITIES FOR YOU AND YOUR CAIRN TERRIER

Happiest when working, Cairn Terriers are intrepid competitors at Obedience trials and Performance events, as well as in the show ring, where their "look at me" attitude wins hearts and ribbons.

Showing Your Cairn Terrier

Since the first group of sportsmen gathered on a Chicago field in the spring of 1874 to compare their dogs' appearance rather than hunting ability, dog shows have grown steadily in popularity in the United States. Last year, for instance, more than 1.3 million dogs competed at over 3,700 all-breed and specialty events. Cairn Terriers, according to statistics, earned 150 of the nearly 22,000 championship titles awarded by the American Kennel Club.

Why have dog shows gained such acceptance with owners and handlers, as well as the public? Many view showing as a competitive activity in which the entire family can take part. Adults and children have an opportunity to make friends and learn new skills as they travel to show sites throughout the country—and even abroad. Some begin as a hobby, perhaps with family pets. However, as they develop a critical eye for their chosen breed, a few persist to become noteworthy breeders. These dedicated individuals continue exhibiting to highlight their kennels' achievements, compare the results of their breeding programs with those of other kennels, and allow fellow breeders to see dogs that might improve their own bloodlines.

If you have an attractive Cairn that conforms to the breed standard (pages 10–11) and has a flashy "Look at me!" attitude, and you think you might enjoy showing him off in the ring, the best way to start is by attending a local show where you can watch experienced handlers and dogs compete in Breed classes, and the more advanced Group and Best in Show judging.

Sponsoring kennel clubs usually have information available on handling classes and match shows that are open to the public. Although

"fun matches" don't award championship points, they provide an excellent arena for preparing your dog and practicing your handling techniques. Also, inquire about becoming a member of the club. By volunteering your talents behind the scenes—or front and center—you'll not only enjoy a greater bond with your pet, but also make friendships that could last a lifetime.

Conformation Classes

Cairn Terriers at least six months old, registered with the AKC, and free of disqualifying faults may enter one of seven regular classes to compete for their championships: Puppy, Twelve-to-Eighteen Month, Novice, Amateur-Owner-Handler, Bred-by-Exhibitor, American-Bred, or Open. Each class is then divided into sections for dogs (males) and bitches (females). Because your Cairn may qualify for more than one class—Puppy and Novice, for example—always select the category in which he stands the best chance of finishing undefeated. (The seven class winners are the only dogs that compete for points at a given show.)

Puppy: Puppies between 6 and 12 months that have not earned their championships compete in this class. Shows with a large number of entries, such as national or regional specialties, often further divide the field into Six-to-Nine Month and Nine-to-Twelve Month Classes. The Puppy Class is ideal for youngsters that are not fully mature or lack experience in the show ring.

Twelve-to-Eighteen Month: This division, a stepping-stone from Puppy to the more advanced classes, is open to all nonchampions between 12 and 18 months. Exhibitors and handlers often choose this class when they expect others to have many entries.

Novice: This class is for dogs that have not yet won three first prizes in Novice, a first place in Bred-by-Exhibitor, American-Bred, or Open, or one or more championship points.

Amateur-Owner-Handler: This new class, beginning in 2009, is for nonchampion dogs that are handled by their amateur owners. No professional handlers or their assistants, or dog judges, are allowed to enter this class.

Bred-by-Exhibitor: Dogs in this class must be owned or co-owned and handled by the breeder or an immediate family member. The Bred-by-Exhibitor Class is an excellent choice for breeders who seek to highlight their kennels' accomplishments.

American-Bred: When dog shows began in the United States, most of the victors came from established British and European bloodlines. To stimulate interest in domestic breeding programs, the AKC initiated a special class for American-bred dogs. Any dog (other than a champion) more than six months, bred and whelped in the United States, is eligible to compete in this category. Many exhibitors and handlers use American-Bred as a transition between Puppy and Open for immature or inexperienced dogs.

Open: Dogs more than six months, including foreign dogs, may compete in the Open Class. Professional handlers exhibit in this category, and dogs must be mature, properly trained and presented, and in top condition.

Winners: If your Cairn won a blue ribbon in his class, you'll return to the ring for the Winners Class. First, all the prizewinning males from each of the classes compete for Winners Dog. This is the only male that receives points toward his championship at the show. The second-place male finisher earns the title Reserve Winners. Next, the female class winners meet to vie for Winners Bitch and Reserve Winners. (The second in the Winners Dog or Winners Bitch class is eligible for and *must* compete for Reserve.)

Best of Breed: After all the regular classes have been judged, the Winners Dog and Winners Bitch, champions of record, and dogs that have completed the requirements for their championships compete for Best of Breed. If your Cairn wins Best of Breed at an all-breed show, he *may* go on to the Terrier Group and, if he wins first place again, he then *must* compete with the six other group winners for the Best in Show award.

Best of Winners: If the Winners Dog or Winners Bitch wins Best of Breed, he or she automatically receives the title Best of Winners. If another dog wins BOB, the two Winners compete against one another for Best of Winners.

Best of Opposite Sex: All entries of the opposite sex to the Best of Breed winner, including the Winners Dog or Winners Bitch, compete for the award Best of Opposite Sex. For example, if the BOB choice is male, all females in the class and the Winners Bitch compete for the BOS title.

Becoming a Champion

To become a champion, your Cairn must earn a total of 15 points. He must win six or more points at two shows—three or more points (called a major) at each show—from two different judges. An additional judge (or judges) must award the remaining points. The number of points your dog can win ranges from zero to five, depending on how many dogs he defeats. If the Winners Dog or Winners Bitch wins Best of Breed, for instance, all Best of Breed competitors are added to the number of defeated dogs to determine the points. If your dog wins the Terrier Group or Best in Show, he takes the highest number of points (usually five) earned in Group or Best in Show competition. An excellent specimen, therefore, can become a champion in three shows, by winning three five-point majors.

Ring Procedure

While you're waiting for your class to begin, watch the current exhibitors from ringside to determine the format of judging at that particular show. Although the procedure may vary from show to show, depending on the size of the ring or its condition, weather, or the number of dogs competing, most judges follow the same pattern with each dog in the class. Typically, you and your dog will enter the ring in "catalog order," according to your armband number and listing in the show catalog. The entire group then gaits around the ring to give the judge a preliminary impression of the dogs' quality. Keep enough space between you and the other handlers so your dogs don't crowd one another. When your turn arrives for individual examination, carefully place your Cairn on the table. You may quickly tidy his coat, but avoid excessive grooming. A Cairn should appear scruffy rather than highly stylized in the ring. The judge will inspect your dog's head and mouth, then proceed down his neck, front, shoulders, body, and hindquarters. If your dog is a male, the judge also will make certain that his testicles have fully descended in the scrotum.

Now your Cairn gets to show off! At the judge's direction, move your dog down and back on a loose lead. When you return to the starting position, your dog should stand at attention (called stacking) with no further handling. You may use a treat or squeaker to attract his attention. To complete your turn, take your Cairn around the ring, once again, to the end of the line of competitors. A judge might encourage a pair of terriers to "spar" in the ring to see how they react. The perfect "spar" is alert, intense, and beautiful—dogs at their natural best. There should be *no* growling, snarling, or snapping. This is not the intent of a spar! At the end of the judging, the first- through fourth-place winners receive their ribbons. When you accept a ribbon—of any color—it's polite and customary to thank the judge. If your Cairn placed in his class, be sure to contact the show photographer to record your victory.

Obedience Competition

Before competitive Obedience began in the United States, most trainers directed their efforts toward the sporting breeds and working dogs. However, a well-known Standard Poodle breeder, Helene Whitehouse Walker, sought to prove the intelligence and trainability of her dogs by devising a basic test that included off-leash heeling, retrieving a dumbbell, sit-stay and down-stay, recall, and broad jump. She also held the first all-breed Obedience test, in 1933, on her estate in upstate New York. Today, the American Kennel Club sponsors more than 2,500 Obedience trials, with nearly 100,000 dogs competing annually. Cairn Terriers have earned titles at all three levels—Novice, Open, and Utility—along with the coveted High in Trial and Obedience Trial Champion awards.

Any AKC-registered dog more than six months old is eligible to compete, including those with limited registrations. If you own an unregistered dog, such as an adopted or rescue dog, contact the AKC for a Purebred Alternative Listing Privilege/Indefinite Listing Privilege (PAL/ILP) number. This allows your dog to enter all Obedience and Performance events. Neutered dogs and those with faults that would disqualify them in the show ring also may participate in these activities.

Getting Started

To learn more about Obedience, attend a local show where you can observe the dogs in the ring. Most kennel clubs offer basic instruction, and you also may find classes given by private trainers, humane organizations, veterinary clinics, or 4-H clubs. Ask to visit one of the classes without your dog. Is it well organized and efficiently run? Do the dogs enjoy working with their owners? Does the instructor clearly explain and demonstrate the exercises? How are the dogs disciplined and rewarded? Are you comfortable with the methods used?

Look for a trainer who has experience with terriers. Cairns are extremely intelligent—they are quick learners that figure out a particular task in the first few minutes of class—but their independence and stubbornness often make them more difficult to work with than other breeds. "The key is to be as tenacious as they

are," explains Lindy Sander, who has owned and trained several high-ranking Obedience Cairns, "and to find out what motivates the individual dog."

Keep in mind that you cannot force your will on a Cairn. "When a Cairn obeys, it's because the dog respects his handler," says veteran breeder Laura DeVincent. "Often, Cairns appear to have 'selective hearing,' and even the best-trained dogs may decide to take off if something more interesting comes along."

When training and competing with a Cairn, try to maintain a sense of humor and don't take their unexpected antics—in class or in the ring—too seriously. Few Cairns will achieve High in Trial, according to Betty Marcum, because they are too mischievous. "It's not that they cannot learn. They are highly intelligent, but just like to play tricks."

Scoring: Obedience exercises are rated on a point scale, based on the judge's mental picture of the ideal performance. "Willingness, enjoyment, and precision" on the part of the dog, and "naturalness, gentleness, and smoothness" in handling are key elements, state the AKC's *Obedience Regulations*. Each dog enters the ring with a perfect score of 200, and then loses points for mistakes like sitting crooked, failing to come when called, or retrieving an incorrect object. Errors in handling result in deductions, as well. Common problems include excessive leash corrections when heeling, using multiple commands, or physically assisting your dog. To earn a qualifying score, called a "leg" toward a title, your dog must achieve half of the required points in each exercise for a minimum of 170 points. After three qualifying scores, from three different judges, your dog receives his Obedience title.

There is no limit to the number of dogs that may qualify at a given show. All dogs that perform correctly earn their green qualifying ribbons and legs toward their titles. In addition, the four dogs with the highest scores in each class receive ribbons and any special prizes offered by the show-giving club. The dog with the highest score, overall, earns High in Trial. If your Cairn qualifies or places in competition, be sure to have the photographer capture the win for your dog's photo album.

Novice: The beginning level, which grants the title Companion Dog (CD), consists of the basic commands that all dogs need to know to be good canine companions. Exercises include on- and off-leash heeling, standing in place for a physical examination by the judge, coming when called, and sitting and lying down for a predetermined length of time.

Open: The next level, which grants the title Companion Dog Excellent (CDX), is more difficult than Novice. Exercises include heeling off leash in different patterns, dropping to the down position during the recall, retrieving a dumbbell on the flat as well as over the high jump, leaping the broad jump, and sitting and lying down while the owner is out of the ring.

Utility: The most difficult level, which challenges even the brightest and most obedient dogs—along with their handlers—grants the title Utility Dog (UD). Exercises include off-leash heeling with hand signals to stand, stay, drop, sit, and come, locating two articles by scent, standing for the judge's examination, and directed retrieving and jumping.

Special Awards: After your dog has earned his CDX and UD titles, he may continue to compete for the Utility Dog Excellent (UDX) award. Your dog must earn qualifying scores in both Open B and Utility B at 10 additional trials. (A minimum number of dogs, according to current AKC rules, must have competed in each class.) Dogs that have earned their UD titles also receive points when they place first or second in Open B or Utility B competition. To qualify as Obedience Trial Champion (OTCh), your dog must have won three first prizes (one each in Open and Utility), from three different judges. He also must have accumulated 100 points, based on the number of dogs he defeated. The letters, OTCh, unlike most Obedience designations, precede your dog's official registered name.

Agility Trials

The sport of Agility originated in 1978 at the renowned Crufts dog show in England. Based on the jumps and barriers of equestrian events, canine Agility proved so popular with spectators that The Kennel Club of Great Britain granted it official status a year later. By the mid-1980s, trainers in the United States had discovered that Agility not only challenged their dogs to master a complicated set of obstacles, but also increased the connection they shared with their pets, as both learned a new set of skills. Since its initiation by the American Kennel Club in 1994, Cairn Terriers have gained titles in all levels of Agility.

Obstacles used in Agility include the dog walk, A-frame, seesaw, tunnels, weave poles, and pause table. Jumps consist of single-, double-, and triple-bar jumps; panel, window, and tire jumps; and the broad jump. Cairns are vigorous and sturdy little terriers that excel at jumping and, of course, going through tunnels. They have an advantage on the narrow dog

Dogs negotiate a series of obstacles, such as this tire jump, against the clock in Agility competition.

walk (an up ramp and ramp connected by boards), and usually hit the obstacles' required "contact zones." However, a trainer who has considerable experience working with small dogs, Gerianne Darnell, has found that some have difficulty scaling the tall A-frame, whereas others are confused by the weave poles—they are set too far apart for the dogs to visualize the pattern of going in and out. Jump heights and time limits are adjusted to give all breeds an equal footing. A special Preferred Class that lowers jump heights by 4 inches (10 cm) and gives additional time to complete the course enables puppies, seniors, and slower breeds to succeed in Agility trials.

Scoring

To achieve a qualifying score, your dog must negotiate the course with speed and accuracy. The judge adds fault points to your dog's score for a variety of penalties: exceeding the course time, refusing an obstacle, crossing incorrectly, or not stepping on the contact zone. You may direct your dog with verbal commands and/or hand signals, but cannot touch or physically assist him in any way. To receive an Agility

title, your dog must execute three qualifying runs under at least two different judges.

Standard

This class comprises jumps, tunnels, and weave poles, along with contact objects, such as the dog walk, A-frame, seesaw, and pause table. Dogs must place at least one paw on the painted contact zones, which are on the up and down sides of the obstacles, and must sit or lie down for at least five seconds on the pause table.

Jumpers with Weaves

A quick-moving course with no contact objects to slow the pace, this class consists of only jumps, tunnels, chutes, and weave poles. Dogs execute between 13 and 20 elements,

depending on the title for which they are competing.

Fifteen and Send Time (FAST)

This class involves negotiating 15 point-valued obstacles, and the Send Bonus. The mandatory single-bar jumps and weave poles are combined with an assortment of jumps and tunnels, as well as a pause table, that have been assigned point values. Dogs must also perform the Send Bonus, in which the handler remains at a specified distance and *sends* the dog to complete the obstacle.

Titles

The AKC awards both regular and Preferred Novice, Open, and Excellent titles in Standard, Jumpers with Weaves, and FAST categories. To receive the Master designation, your dog must earn 10 qualifying scores after achieving the Excellent title. The top-level Master Agility Champion (MACH) award is given to dogs that earn at least 750 points and 20 qualifying scores in Excellent Standard *and* Excellent Jumpers with Weaves classes.

Earthdog Tests

Designed for small terriers and Dachshunds, Earthdog tests assess your Cairn's instinctive and trained hunting and working abilities in the pursuit of underground quarry. The man-made "dens" consist of 9-inch (23-cm) square liners set into trenches in the ground and covered with brush and other materials to look as natural as possible. At the end of the tunnel, which is scented like an actual den, is a securely caged pair of adult rats or artificial quarry. The object of the test is to follow the correct scent line to the entrance, enter the den, and then "work" the prey by barking, growling, digging, scratching, or lunging to show interest. Many Cairns, though, are "silent workers," according to Joyce Moore, an AKC-licensed Earthdog judge who also trains her Cairns for Earthdog events. "Barking is not always heard from the tunnel when the dog reaches the rat. Cairns are more inclined to dig, scratch, bite at the bars, and whine, which nonetheless constitute work from a judging standpoint. Getting to the quarry and staring at it *does not* qualify as work." Also, when dropped at the start of the test, "Cairns don't charge the tunnel, but are more apt to follow the scent trail and check out the entrance before going in," she adds. "Once in the tunnel, though, they are very fast in negotiating the turns and obstacles to reach the quarry."

The key to preparing for Earthdog trials is to begin when your Cairn is a puppy, with practice "hunting" sessions in the backyard. Moore suggests using a straight piece of PVC pipe, about 10 feet (3 m) long, to accustom the puppy to entering and traversing a dark, narrow space with confidence. "His favorite toy should await him at the other end," she explains, "as you tease him into a sense of accomplishment over finding the 'quarry,' and putting up a 'good old terrier tug' to 'shake his timbers.' The puppy will begin to revel in this game, displaying his natural instincts and the heart and soul of why he was bred to be here." However, never overtrain your Cairn or he will become bored and refuse to participate. Also, never force your dog into the tunnel, admonishes Moore. "This has to be a fun activity that allows him to exercise those instincts that were bred in many, many years ago."

Titles

The noncredit test, Introduction to Quarry, is for novice dogs that have had no prior exposure to tunnel work. Entering a simple 10-foot passageway with a 90-degree turn, your dog must locate and then work the quarry for the specified length of time. A scent trail leads into the tunnel and to the caged rats. The Junior Earthdog (JE) test is similar to the first test, but the tunnel is longer and contains three 90-degree angles. In the Senior Earthdog (SE) test, your dog must locate the quarry in a more complex den, with a scented false den and exit. In addition to correctly locating and working the quarry, your dog must leave the den on command. The most difficult test, Master Earthdog (ME), is designed to simulate an authentic hunting situation. Your dog must distinguish the correct entrance from an unscented false passage, reach the quarry through a tunnel that consists of an obstacle and a constriction, and work the quarry as

required. Dogs perform this test in pairs, with one dog staked near the entrance while the other works the quarry. After finishing in the den, the first dog changes places with the waiting dog. Dogs must qualify twice for the JE title, three times for the SE title, and four times for the ME title, from at least two different judges.

Flyball

The fast-paced canine sport of Flyball originated nearly 40 years ago when a group of trainers in Southern California threw tennis balls to their dogs at the end of a hurdle-racing event. Flyball gained national attention in the late 1970s after the inventor of the first ball-launching box, Herbert Wagner, gave a demonstration on *The Tonight Show* starring Johnny Carson. The first tournament was held in 1983, and the following year a dozen teams from the Toronto-Detroit area formed the North American Flyball Association (NAFA). Today, more than 16,000 dogs and over 700 dog-training clubs compete under NAFA guidelines.

Flyball is a relay-style race with two teams, each consisting of four dogs, running side by side against one another. Each dog runs the length of the 51-foot (15-m) track, jumping hurdles spaced 10 feet (3 m) apart. The height of the hurdles is 4 inches (10 cm) less than the shortest dog's height at the withers, so including a small dog lowers the jump height for the entire team. At the end of the line, the dog steps on a spring-loaded box that releases a tennis ball. The dog grabs the ball as quickly as possible and returns across the hurdles to the starting line. Only when the previous dog crosses the line does the next dog take his turn. The first team that finishes, without errors, wins the heat and progresses to the next round in the tournament. The top Flyball team in the United States holds the NAFA World Record at 15.43 seconds!

Scoring

Each member of the winning team receives points, based on the time it takes all four dogs to accurately complete the course. Teams that finish in less than 32 seconds give each dog 1 point; 28 seconds, 5 points; and 24 seconds, 25 points. Tournaments use an electronic judging system, equipped with lights and infrared timing sensors, to record starts, finishes, and race times to one-thousandth of a second.

Titles

NAFA awards titles based on the number of points a dog accumulates throughout his com-

petitive career. Dogs that earn 20 points receive the title Flyball Dog (FD), followed by Flyball Dog Excellent (FDX) and Flyball Dog Champion (FDCh). At 5,000 points, dogs earn Flyball Master (FM), followed by Flyball Master Excellent (FMX) and Flyball Master Champion (FMCh). At 20,000 points, dogs earn ONYX, followed by Flyball Grand Champion (FGDCh) and—for dogs with at least 100,000 points—the Hobbes award. To date, Allie Moran, owned by Mike Moran, is the top Cairn Terrier in Flyball, having retired at the ONYX level with more than 22,000 points.

Rally

Similar to rally-style auto racing, in which drivers proceed at their own pace, following a set of written directions to reach their destination, this newest AKC event began in 2005 as a bridge between the Canine Good Citizen (CGC) Program and formal Obedience and Agility competition. The Rally judge sets up the course for each trial, and posts a map at ringside. You may walk the course ahead of time—without your dog—to become familiar with the required exercises. After the judge gives the "Forward!" command, you and your dog execute a sequence of marked stations that features both stationary and moving skills, such as Sit and Down, turns in different directions, changes of pace, and moving around pylons in specific patterns. You're expected to complete the course at a brisk pace, with no further intervention from the judge. In Rally, unlike Obedience, you may give your Cairn multiple commands, encouragement, and praise. Any command deemed too harsh is penalized, and touching or physical corrections are not allowed.

Scoring

Each dog enters the ring with a perfect score of 100 points, then loses from 1 to 10 points for mistakes like a poor sit, touching a pylon, knocking over a jump, or not performing the skill. Handler errors, such as using a tight leash, giving a loud command, or poor teamwork, also result in deductions. Teams are timed as well, but course times are used only as tiebreakers in the event that more than one team receives the same point score. After three qualifying scores, from two different judges, your dog receives his Rally title.

Titles

Novice: The beginning level, which grants the title Rally Novice (RN), consists of 10 to 15 stations, with three to five stationary skills like *Sit* or *Down*, that show your dog's knowledge of basic commands. The entire Novice course is performed on leash, and perfect heel position is not required.

Advanced: The next level, Rally Advanced (RA), is progressively more difficult. The course includes 12 to 17 stations, three to seven stationary exercises, three advanced skills, and a jump (broad, high, or bar jump). The advanced course is performed off leash.

Excellent: The most difficult level, Rally Excellent (RE), requires 15 to 20 stations, three to seven stationary exercises, three advanced-level and two excellent-level skills, and two jumps. It also includes Honor Exercises, in which your dog must remain in an assigned *sit* or *down* position—without moving—as a second "running dog" completes his turn at the course.

Special Awards: The title Rally Advanced Excellent (RAE) is awarded to dogs that qualify 10 times in both Rally Advanced B and Rally Excellent B at the same trial.

Tracking Tests

Developed in the 1930s as a component of the Utility Dog test, tracking measures a dog's ability to recognize and follow the scent of a human track layer. To navigate the terrain, which may include vegetation, gravel, sand, concrete, or other surfaces, your dog must work in a tracking harness on a 20- to 40-foot leash. You may give verbal commands and encouragement, but signals or movements that guide your dog to a particular location are prohibited. The AKC calls Tracking "a team sport in the truest sense." Fay Fowler Gross, who began teaching her Cairns to track in the early 1970s, agrees: "In every other area of training, the handler basically runs the show. This cannot be done in Tracking. Here, success means putting your faith in your dog to make the correct decisions. If you have gotten your point across to your dog that the scent at the starting flag is the one to pursue, all you have to do is follow along behind."

Close to Ground

Cairns, whose scenting ability rivals that of any working dog, do very well in Tracking, according to Gross. "A short-legged breed like the Cairn is already close to the ground, so he can investigate areas where larger dogs can't go. His coat allows him to penetrate dense brush, as it protects him from harsh weather conditions. Cairns are agile and can climb almost as well as a cat. Many love to swim, too, so crossing water is rarely a problem."

To begin training, suggests Gross, place your dog in a harness with the leash attached. With another handler holding your dog, play with him to build enthusiasm. Then, quickly run out of sight and hide. The handler gradually lets out the leash, while giving the command, "Track!" or "Find it!" Remain hidden until your dog finds you, and praise him profusely when he succeeds. "Although many dogs begin looking and air scenting, they quickly put their noses to the ground and actually track where their owners have walked," says Gross. Searching for a favorite person or article is the best way to keep the dogs interested. "So many people think they have to do regulation tracks all the time," she adds. "I do them only occasionally. Remember, we are not teaching the dog a thing he does not already know—the handlers are the ones who need to learn to follow their dogs."

A short-legged breed, like the Cairn, excels at Tracking. This puppy has already discovered how to use his nose to follow a scent.

Scoring: To pass this test, your dog must follow the scent of the track layer and locate the article, or articles, he dropped. The article(s) must be presented to the judge at the end of the test. There is no time limit for finding the article(s), but your dog must appear to be actively searching. He earns his title by successfully completing one track.

Titles: AKC titles include Tracking Dog (TD), Tracking Dog Excellent (TDX), and Variable Surface Tracking (VST). To receive the title Champion Tracker (CT), your dog must earn all three tracking awards. The letters, CT, precede your dog's official registered name.

To learn more about dog shows, Obedience competition, Performance events, and other activities you can share with your Cairn Terrier, contact the American Kennel Club, your local kennel or training club, or the Cairn Terrier Club of America (see Information, page 90).

Kennel Clubs

American Kennel Club
260 Madison Avenue
New York, NY 10016
www.akc.org

Canadian Kennel Club
200 Ronson Drive, Suite 400
Etobicoke, Ontario, Canada
M9W 5Z9
www.ckc.ca

The Kennel Club (UK)
1 - 5 Clarges Street
Piccadilly, London, England
W1J 8AB
thekennelclub.org.uk

United Kennel Club, Inc.
100 East Kilgore Road
Kalamazoo, MI 49002-5584
www.ukcdogs.com

Cairn Terrier Club of America, Inc.
www.cairnterrier.org

The Foundation of the Cairn
   Terrier Club of America, Inc.
ctca-foundation.org

Cairn Terrier Club of Canada
www.cairnterrierclub.ca

The Cairn Terrier Club (UK)
www.thecairnterrierclub.co.uk

Cairn Terrier Books

Birch, Ron and Brenda. *Cairn Terriers (Pet Owner's Guide)*. Lydney, UK: Ringpress Books, 2000.

Cairn Terrier Champions: 1952–1986, 1987–1996, 1997–2004. Incline Village, NV: Camino Books, Inc., multiple editions.

Carter, Christine. *The Cairn Terrier*. Neptune City, NJ: TFH Publications, Inc., 1996.

Jamieson, Robert. *Cairn Terrier (Kennel Club Dog Breed Series)*. Freehold, NJ: Kennel Club Books, 2004.

Marcum, Betty E. *The New Cairn Terrier*. New York, NY: Howell Book House, Inc., 1995.

McCormack, Erliss. *Cairn Terriers*. Neptune City, NJ: TFH Publications, Inc., multiple editions.

Murray, Sandra. *The New Owner's Guide to Cairn Terriers*. Neptune City, NJ: TFH Publications, Inc., 2004.

Antique, Out of Print, and Hard to Find Books

Ash, Edward C. *Dogs: Their History and Development*. London: Ernest Benn Limited, 1927.

Cooke, Ryan and Cynthia. *The Cairn Terrier in Canada, Vol. 1: A Compilation of Canadian Cairn Terrier Records 1920–1995*. East St. Paul, MB, Canada, 1997.

Gordon, John. *All About the Cairn Terrier*. New York, NY: Viking Press, 1988.

Jacobi, Girard A. *Your Cairn Terrier*. Fairfax, VA: Denlinger's Publishers, Ltd., 1976.

Marvin, John T. *The New Complete Cairn Terrier*. New York, NY: Howell Book House, Inc., 1987.

Rogers, Mrs. Byron. *Cairn and Sealyham Terriers*. New York, NY: Robert M. McBride & Company, 1922.

Ross, Florence M. *The Cairn Terrier*. Manchester, England: "Our Dogs" Publishing Company Limited, 1926.

Vaughn, Clarence F., and David Fee. *The Cairn Terrier in America*. Scottsdale, AZ: Privately published, 1994.

Whitehead, Hector F. *Cairn Terriers*. New York, NY: Arco Publishing, Inc., 1976.

General Dog Books

Alderton, David. *The Dog Care Manual*. Hauppauge, NY: Barron's Educational Series, Inc., 1986.

American Kennel Club. *The Complete Dog Book*. New York, NY: Howell Book House, Inc., 2006.

Eldridge, Debra M., D.V.M., Liisa D. Carlson, D.V.M., Delbert G. Carlson, D.V.M., James M. Giffin, M.D., Beth Adelman (Editor). *Dog Owner's Home Veterinary Handbook*. New York, NY: Howell Book House, Inc., 2007.

Kalstone, Shirlee and Walter McNamara. *First Aid For Dogs*. New York, NY: Arco Publishing, Inc., 1980.

Lehman, Patricia F. *Your Healthy Puppy*. Neptune City, NJ: TFH Publications, Inc., 1998.

Lewis, Lon D., D.V.M., Ph.D., et al. *Small Animal Clinical Nutrition IV*. Topeka, KS: Mark Morris Associates, 2000.

Migliorini, Mario. *Dig In! Earthdog Training Made Easy*. New York, NY: Howell Book House, Inc., 1997.

Pinney, Chris C., D.V.M. *Caring for Your Older Dog*. Hauppauge, NY: Barron's Educational Series, Inc., 1995.

Rice, Dan, D.V.M. *The Complete Book of Dog Breeding*. Hauppauge, NY: Barron's Educational Series, Inc., 1996.

Streitferdt, Dr. Uwe. *Healthy Dog, Happy Dog: A Complete Guide to Dog Diseases and Their Treatments*. Hauppauge, NY: Barron's Educational Series, Inc., 1994.

Walkowicz, Chris, and Bonnie Wilcox, D.V.M. *Successful Dog Breeding, The Complete Handbook of Canine Midwifery*. New York, NY: Prentice Hall Press, 1985.

Publications available from the Cairn Terrier Club of America

Cairn Terrier Grooming, Start to Finish
Clarification and Amplification of the Standard
Visualization of the Cairn Standard
The Cairn Terrier, by Baroness Burton
Meet the Cairn Terrier
CTCA Yearbooks 1978–1992

Dog Magazines

AKC Gazette
American Kennel Club
260 Madison Avenue, 19th Floor
New York, NY 10016
www.akc.org

Bloodlines
United Kennel Club, Inc.
100 East Kilgore Road
Kalamazoo, MI 49002-5584
www.ukcdogs.com

Dog Fancy and *Dog World*
P.O. Box 6050
Mission Viejo, CA 92690-6050
www.dogchannel.com/dog-magazines/
   dogfancy/default.aspx
www.dogchannel.com/dog-magazines/
   dogworld/default.aspx

Dogs In Canada
Apex Publishing, Ltd.
200 Ronson Drive, Suite 401
Etobicoke, Ontario, Canada
M9W 5Z9
www.dogsincanada.com

The Whole Dog Journal
P.O. Box 1349
Oroville, CA 95965
www.whole-dog-journal.com

Videos

Movement in the Cairn
Cairn Terrier Club of America
www.cairnterrier.org

Organizations and Suppliers

AKC Canine Health Foundation
P.O. Box 900061
Raleigh, NC 27675-9061
www.akcchf.org

American Working Terrier Association
www.dirt-dog.com/awta/index.cfm

Canine Eye Registration Foundation, Inc.
   (CERF)
VMDB/CERF
P.O. Box 3007
Urbana, IL 61803-3007
www.vmdb.org/cerf.html

Canine Good Citizen (CGC) Program
American Kennel Club
8051 Arco Corporate Drive, Suite 100
Raleigh, NC 27617-3390
www.akc.org

Institute for Genetic Disease Control
P.O. Box 177
Warner, NH 03278
www.gdcinstitute.org

North American Flyball Association, Inc.
1400 West Devon Avenue, #512
Chicago, IL 60660
www.flyball.org

The Orthopedic Foundation for Animals, Inc.
2300 E. Nifong Boulevard
Columbia, MO 65201-3806
www.offa.org

United States Dog Agility Association
   (USDAA)
P.O. Box 850955
Richardson, TX 75085-0955
www.usdaa.com

Important Note

This pet owner's guide tells the reader how to buy and care for a Cairn Terrier. The author and the publisher consider it important to point out that the advice given in the book is meant primarily for normally developed puppies from a good breeder—that is, dogs of excellent physical health and good temperament.

Anyone who adopts a fully grown dog should be aware that the animal has already formed his basic impressions of human beings. The new owner should watch the animal carefully, including his behavior toward humans, and should meet the previous owner. If the dog comes from a shelter, it may be possible to get some information on the dog's background and characteristics there. There are dogs that for whatever reason behave in an unnatural manner or may even bite. Under no circumstances should a known "biter" or an otherwise ill-tempered dog be adopted or purchased as a pet or show prospect.

Caution is further advised in the association of children with dogs, in meeting with other dogs, and in exercising the dog without a leash.

Even well-behaved and carefully supervised dogs sometimes do damage to someone else's property or cause accidents. It is therefore in the owner's interest to be adequately insured against such possibilities, and we strongly urge all dog owners to purchase a liability policy that covers their dog.

Acknowledgments

The author would like to express her appreciation to the following contributors: Barbara Cole, Gerianne Darnell, Laura DeVincent, Diane Eatherton, Fay Fowler Gross, Louise Hooper, Betty E. Marcum, Joyce Moore, Lindy Sander, Sandra Speicher, and Natalie H. Winslow.

Photo Credits

Cheryl A. Ertelt: pages 9, 28, 29, 35, 63, 68, 93; Jean M. Fogle: pages 4, 6, 10, 18, 22, 26, 30, 43, 47, 71, 76, 83, 84, 85, 86, 87; Isabelle Français: pages 5, 12, 14, 24, 25, 27, 32, 33, 34, 39, 40, 44, 46, 52, 54, 59, 60, 62, 65, 89; Karen Hudson: page 80; Pets by Paulette: pages 2–3, 8, 13, 17, 21, 23, 31, 41, 42, 45, 48, 49, 53, 57, 63, 66, 70, 73, 77, 78.

Cover Photos

Front cover: Shutterstock; inside front cover: Pets by Paulette; inside back cover: Jean M. Fogle; back cover: Isabelle Francais.

The first edition of *Cairn Terriers (A Complete Pet Owner's Manual)* was named "Best Short Book" (under 100 pages) by the Dog Writers Association of America, Inc.

A Note About Pronouns

Many dog lovers feel that the pronoun "it" is not appropriate when referring to a beloved pet. For this reason, Cairn Terriers are described as "he" throughout this book, unless the topic specifically relates to female dogs. This by no means infers any preference, nor should it be taken as an indication that either sex is problematic.

About the Author

Patricia F. Lehman is a freelance writer, specializing in the topic of dogs and their care. Her work has appeared in a variety of canine magazines, newspapers, and newsletters. Her books include *The Miniature Pinscher: King of Toys* and *Your Healthy Puppy*. She is a member and former treasurer of the Dog Writers Association of America, Inc. She has won the Iams Company's Eukanuba Nutrition Award for the best article on canine nutrition, as well as four DWAA Honorable Mention certificates for excellence in dog writing. She also holds the designation Small Animal Dietitian from Hill's Pet Products. A graduate of the University of Delaware, the author lives with her family in Wilmington, Delaware.

All inquiries should be addressed to:
Barron's Educational Series, Inc.
250 Wireless Boulevard
Hauppauge, NY 11788
www.barronseduc.com

ISBN-13: 978-0-7641-4102-7
ISBN-10: 0-7641-4102-3

Library of Congress Catalog Card No. 2008030021

Library of Congress Cataloging-in-Publication Data
Lehman, Patricia F.
  Cairn terriers / Patricia Lehman.
    p. cm. — (A complete pet owner's manual)
  Includes index.
  ISBN-13: 978-0-7641-4102-7
  ISBN-10: 0-7641-4102-3
  1. Cairn terrier. I. Title.

SF429.C3L44 2009
636.755—dc22   2008030021

Printed in China
9 8 7 6 5 4 3 2 1